PEARSON

my **Student** JOURNAL

This Student Journal belongs to

_____

PEARSON

Boston, Massachusetts
Chandler, Arizona
Glenview, Illinois
Upper Saddle River, New Jersey

myWorld Geography™

Acknowledgments appear on page 304, which constitute an extension of this copyright page.

ISBN-13:   978-0-13-363804-2
ISBN-10:   0-13-363804-9
6 7 8 9 10 V069 14 13

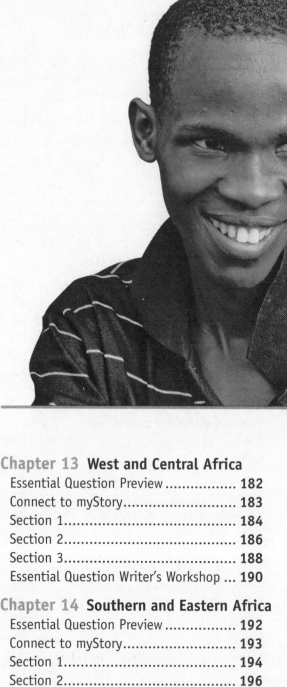

How to Use This Book

The *myWorld Geography Student Journal* is a tool to help you process and record what you have learned from the Student Edition of *myWorld Geography*. As you complete the activities and essays in your Journal, you will be creating your own personal resource for reviewing the concepts, key terms, and maps from *myWorld Geography*. The Journal worksheets and writing exercises focus on the Essential Question, helping you uncover the relevance of each chapter to your life.

The **Essential Question Preview** will help you understand the chapter you are about to read. Begin with Connect to Your Life to find ways to relate the issues and principles of the Essential Questions to your life—your family, school, or community. Next, Connect to the Chapter invites you to flip through the chapter and chart your predictions on how the Essential Question relates to the countries in each chapter.

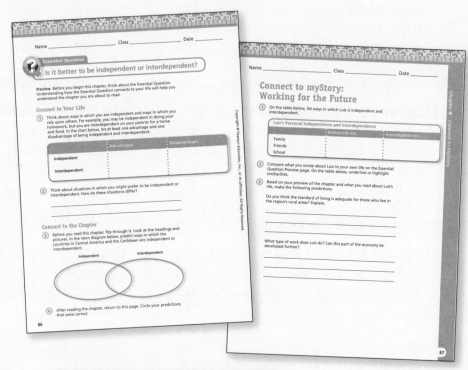

You will build your Map Skills and make the maps your own by locating features on the line maps in **Take Notes.** You can synthesize concepts and create a detailed visual study guide by filling in the illustrated graphic organizers in Take Notes. Each Take Notes page ends with an exercise that helps you draw conclusions about the Essential Question.

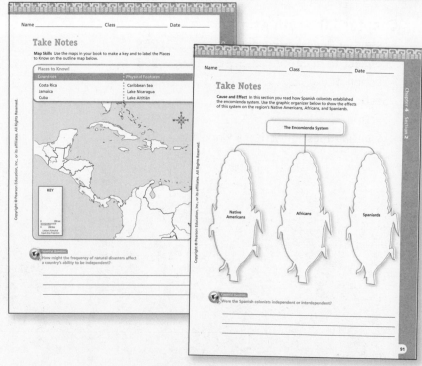

Name _____ Class _____ Date _____

Essential Question | Writer's Workshop

Is it better to be independent or interdependent?

Prepare to Write
Throughout this chapter, you have explored the Essential Question in your text, journal, and On Assignment at myWorldGeography.com. Using what you have learned, write an essay in which you explain whether it is better for Central American and Caribbean nations to be independent or interdependent.

Workshop Skill: Write an Introduction and Thesis Statement
First, review the four types of essays. Then decide which type is best suited to the ideas you wish to express. Which type of essay have you chosen?

_____

Develop your thesis, which is your response to the Essential Question. Begin by reviewing your notes. To help you choose a position, list reasons that support each position in the table below.

Independent	Interdependent

Write the position you have chosen below, along with the three strongest reasons that support it. Note at least one fact or example for each reason.

Position	
Supporting Reasons	Facts and/or Examples

94

Write Your Thesis Statement
Your thesis statement states your position and three reasons that support it. The thesis statement will be the last sentence(s) in your introductory paragraph. For example: *Independence is essential for Central American and Caribbean nations because*

_____, _____, and _____

If your sentence is too long, place your reasons in a second sentence. For example: *Independence is essential for Central American and Caribbean countries. This is true because*

_____, _____, and _____

Now write your thesis statement:

Write Your Introduction
The first paragraph of an essay introduces the topic to the reader. An introduction has three parts:

1. A statement indicating what the essay is about.

Example *Independence and interdependence are characteristics that* _____

2. An indication of why the subject or issue is important.

Example *Understanding a particular nation's independence or*

interdependence is essential to understanding _____

3. A thesis statement.

Write your introductory sentence: _____

State the issue's importance: _____

Write your thesis statement, including three supporting arguments: _____

Draft Your Essay
Introduction: Rewrite your introductory paragraph on your own paper.
Body Paragraphs: Develop each argument to support your position in a separate paragraph. Include details and examples.
Conclusion: Summarize your arguments. When you have finished, proofread your essay.

95

The **Essential Question Writer's Workshop** provides you an end-of-chapter opportunity to show your understanding of chapter content by writing about the Essential Question. Each Workshop features instruction and practice with one of the skills you will need to write an essay and express your ideas. The Writer's Workshop exercises and the activities you have completed in your Journal will help you draw conclusions about the Chapter Essential Question.

Name _____ Class _____ Date _____

Word Wise

Crossword Puzzle The clues describe key terms from this section. Fill in the numbered *Across* boxes with the correct key terms. Then, do the same with the Down clues.

Across
1. a Muslim house of worship
2. a culture that has writing and where people do many different types of jobs
3. a group with less than half of the population

Down
4. worshipping only one god
5. the holy book of Islam
6. an all-powerful leader who has complete control over a nation
7. an Islamic political and religious leader

216

Name _____ Class _____ Date _____

Word Wise

Word Bank Choose one word from the word bank to fill in each blank. When you have finished, you will have a short summary of important ideas from the section.

Word Bank
isthmus
tourism
hurricanes
biodiversity
deforestation

Central America is located on a(n) _____ that is rich in _____. However, _____ has seriously reduced the number of native plants and animals in the region.

Although Central America has its share of natural disasters such as _____, many people vacation in Central American countries. As a result, _____ contributes to the economies of these nations. Plantations, or large commercial farms, are another important part of the region's economy.

The **Word Wise** exercises give you the chance to really get to know and explore the key terms through word maps, crossword puzzles, and other game formats.

Core Concepts 1.1: Word Wise

Word Bank Choose one word from the word bank to fill in each blank.
When you have finished, you will have a short summary of important ideas
from the section.

Word Bank

geography   cardinal directions

sphere   latitude

degrees   longitude

hemispheres

North, south, east, and west are the _____. People use

them to describe the location of places. They also use imaginary lines drawn

across the surface of Earth. Lines that run north to south are called lines of

_____, while those that run east to west are lines of

_____. These lines are measured in units called

_____. Each one of these lines goes in a circle around Earth,

which has the shape of a _____. The equator is the east-

west line that runs across the center of Earth. The equator divides our planet

into two equal _____, or halves. The study of Earth and its

human and non-human features is called _____.

Core Concepts 1.2: Word Wise

Words In Context For each question below, write an answer that shows your understanding of the boldfaced key term.

1 How does **absolute location** differ from **relative location**?

_____

_____

2 What does the geographic theme of **place** describe about a location?

_____

_____

3 The Midwest is one **region** of the United States. What characteristics make it a **region**?

_____

_____

4 How can you see the theme of **movement** in a city like Washington, D.C.?

_____

_____

5 How does **human-environment interaction** affect your life?

_____

_____

Name _____ Class _____ Date _____

Core Concepts 1.3: Word Wise

Vocabulary Quiz Show Some quiz shows ask a question and expect the contestant to give the answer. In other shows, the contestant is given an answer and must supply the question. If the blank is in the question column, write the question that would result in the answer given. If the question is supplied, write the appropriate answer.

QUESTION

1. What do you call photographs taken from airplanes or helicopters?

2. _____

3. What is the name for a computer-based system that stores and uses information linked to geographic locations?

4. _____

5. What do you call a flat map of Earth's round surface?

6. _____

ANSWER

1. _____

2. scale

3. _____

4. satellite images

5. _____

6. distortion

Name _____   Class _____   Date _____

Core Concepts 1.4: Word Wise

Crossword Puzzle The clues describe key terms from this section. Fill in the numbered *Across* boxes with the correct key terms. Then, do the same with the *Down* clues.

Across	Down
1. a map that shows an enlarged view of one part of the main map	4. a standard map diagram that shows the cardinal directions
2. the map part that shows how much space on the map represents a given distance	
3. the map part that shows what the map symbols mean	

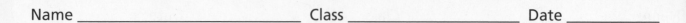

Core Concepts 1.5: Word Wise

Sentence Builder Complete the sentences using the information you learned in this section. Be sure to include terminal punctuation.

1. **Elevation** refers to the _____

_____

_____

2. A **special-purpose map** may show such things as _____

_____

_____

3. A **political map** of your state would show _____

_____

_____

4. A **physical map** shows _____

_____

_____

Sum It Up

Map Your Classroom Apply what you have learned about the tools of
geography to your life by drawing a map of your classroom. Include a key
and a compass rose. Use a tape measure or yardstick to make a scale bar.
Draw a locator map to show the location of your classroom within your
school.

Use the theme of place to describe the relative location of your classroom.

_____

_____

_____

Core Concepts 2.1: Word Wise

Sentence Builder Complete the sentences using the information you learned in this section. Include terminal punctuation.

① Earth moves around the sun in an **orbit** that takes _____

days to _____

② The months of _____ and _____ have

the _____ and _____ **equinoxes,**

which are _____

③ It takes Earth _____ to complete a **revolution,** which is

_____

④ The _____ and _____ **solstices,** which

occur during the months of _____ and

_____, are _____

⑤ Earth _____ on its **axis,** which is an imaginary

_____

Name _____ Class _____ Date _____

Core Concepts 2.2: Word Wise

Words In Context For each question below, write an answer that shows your understanding of the boldfaced key term.

(1) How does Earth's **rotation** differ from its revolution?

_____

_____

_____

(2) Why does Earth have multiple **time zones**?

_____

_____

_____

Core Concepts 2.3: Word Wise

Vocabulary Quiz Show Some quiz shows ask a question and expect the contestant to give the answer. In other shows, the contestant is given an answer and must supply the question. If the blank is in the question column, write the question that would result in the answer given. If the question is supplied, write the appropriate answer.

QUESTION	ANSWER
(1) _____	(1) core
(2) What do you call the thick layer of gases that surround our planet and make life possible?	(2) _____
(3) _____	(3) mantle
(4) What gets created by the physical processes that change Earth's surface by pushing its crust up or wearing it down?	(4) _____
(5) _____	(5) crust

Core Concepts 2.4: Word Wise

Crossword Puzzle The clues describe key terms from this section. Fill in the numbered *Across* boxes with the correct key terms. Then, do the same with the *Down* clues.

Across	Down
1. when water, ice, or wind remove small pieces of rock	5. flat plains formed on the seabed where a river deposits material over many years
2. a stretch of low land between mountains, often formed by a river	6. a large area of flat or gently rolling land
3. occurs when running water picks up material from one place and leaves it in another	7. wearing down rocks by chemical or mechanical means
4. a high area with a flat top and at least one steep side	

Core Concepts 2.5: Word Wise

Word Bank Choose one word from the word bank to fill in each blank. When you have finished, you will have a short summary of important ideas from the section.

Word Bank

magma   plates

faults   plate tectonics

Earth's crust is broken up into many huge blocks called

_____. According to the theory of _____,

these blocks slide and grind against one another. The places where their

edges meet are called _____, and this is where volcanoes

often form. When a volcano erupts, _____, which is melted

rock from deep within Earth, pours out onto the crust. Once it comes out of

the volcano, it is called lava.

Name _____ Class _____ Date _____

Sum It Up

Label the Diagram Mark these physical features in the appropriate areas on the diagram below.

river valley   plateau
delta   mountains

Name three forces that create these features. Explain how each one works.

_____

_____

_____

Name _____ Class _____ Date _____

Core Concepts 3.1: Word Wise

Sentence Builder Complete the sentences using the information you learned in this section. Include terminal punctuation.

(1) Types of **precipitation** include _____

_____

(2) **Climate** describes the average _____ and other factors in

an area _____

(3) Listening to a **weather** forecast lets you know _____

_____

(4) On a climate graph, the line labeled **temperature** shows _____

_____

Name _____   Class _____   Date _____

Core Concepts 3.2: Word Wise

Crossword Puzzle The clues describe key terms from this section. Fill in the numbered *Across* boxes with the correct key terms. Then, do the same with the *Down* clues.

Across	Down
1. name for the areas that lie north of the Arctic Circle and south of the Antarctic Circle	5. height above sea level
2. term describing the area between high and low latitudes	6. another name for the middle latitudes
3. another name for the high latitudes	7. term for the area between the Tropic of Cancer and the Tropic of Capricorn
4. where the sun stays overhead or nearly overhead all year long	

Core Concepts 3.3: Word Wise

Word Bank Choose one word from the word bank to fill in each blank. When you have finished, you will have a short summary of important ideas from the section.

Word Bank

evaporation   water cycle

Water, in one form or another, is constantly moving from Earth's

surface into the atmosphere and back to the surface. This process is called

the _____ and consists of four stages. The first stage is

_____, when water from a puddle, river, or sea changes

into water vapor. Then it rises into the sky. The vapor condenses into clouds

high in the atmosphere. The vapor eventually cools, forms droplets or

snowflakes, and falls to the ground as rain or snow. The precipitation is then

absorbed by the ground or a body of water, where it will start the water

cycle all over again.

Core Concepts 3.4: Word Wise

Words In Context For each question below, write an answer that shows your understanding of the boldfaced key term.

(1) How might people prepare for a **tropical cyclone**?

_____

_____

_____

(2) Why do people fear **tornadoes**?

_____

_____

_____

(3) What is one reason that precipitation is so heavy in the **intertropical convergence zone**?

_____

_____

_____

(4) What weather conditions would you expect to see if a **hurricane** struck your region?

_____

_____

_____

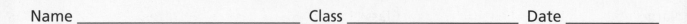

Name _____ Class _____ Date _____

Core Concepts 3.5: Word Wise

Word Bank Choose one word from the word bank to fill in each blank.
When you have finished, you will have a short summary of important ideas
from the section.

Word Bank

tropical wet	tropical wet and dry
semiarid	arid
maritime	humid subtropical
subarctic	tundra

Earth has many climate types. Each one has a unique set of temperature

ranges, kinds of precipitation, and prevailing winds. Areas near the Equator

have a _____ climate, which is a type of climate much

wetter than the _____ climate. The desert

_____ climate is found in places where there it is generally

hot with little precipitation. The _____ climate has wet

summers and dry winters affected by the movement of the sun and shifting

bands of rain over the Equator.

In cold, dry areas in far northern North America and Asia, the

_____ climate is characterized by cool summers and bitterly

cold, dry winters. _____ climates also have cool summers

and very cold winters but have more precipitation, which allows pine trees

to grow.

In areas where moist winds bring precipitation from the ocean, the

climate is described as _____. In these areas, winters are

mild and summers are hot. This is different from the _____

climate, which also exists where winds are moist. However, this type of

climate has cool summers.

Name _____ Class _____ Date _____

Core Concepts 3.6: Word Wise

Vocabulary Quiz Show Some quiz shows ask a question and expect the contestant to give the answer. In other shows, the contestant is given an answer and must supply the question. If the blank is in the question column, write the question that would result in the answer given. If the question is supplied, write the appropriate answer.

QUESTION

1. What do you call a grassland found in a tropical area with dry spells?

2. _____

3. What is an interdependent community formed by plants and animals sharing an environment?

4. _____

ANSWER

1. _____

2. deciduous trees

3. _____

4. coniferous trees

Sum It Up

Make Connections Use the text and maps from this section to fill in the circles of this concept web. Describe the features of a tropical wet and dry climate.

(1) Temperature

(2) Latitudes and hemispheres

(3) Precipitation

(4) Air patterns

(5) Connected ecosystems

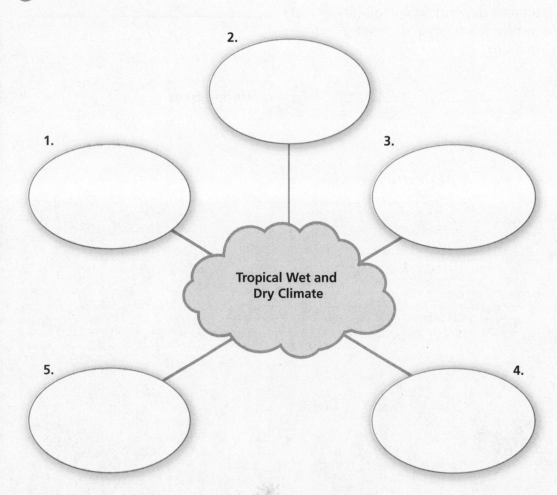

2.

1.

3.

Tropical Wet and Dry Climate

5.

4.

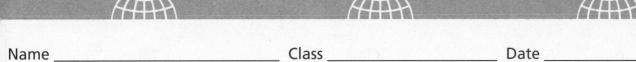

Name _____ Class _____ Date _____

Core Concepts 4.1: Word Wise

Words In Context For each question below, write an answer that shows your understanding of the boldfaced key term.

① Why are trees considered a **renewable resource**?

_____

_____

② What makes water an important **natural resource**?

_____

_____

③ Where do **fossil fuels** get their name?

_____

_____

④ Name three factors that the **nonrenewable resources** of coal and petroleum have in common.

_____

_____

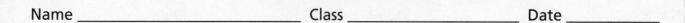

Name _____ Class _____ Date _____

Core Concepts 4.2: Word Wise

Word Map Follow the model below to make a word map. The key term *colonization* is in the center oval. Write the definition in your own words at the upper left. In the upper right, list Characteristics, which means words or phrases that relate to the term. At the lower left list Noncharacteristics, which means words and phrases that would not be associated with it. In the lower right, draw a picture of the key term or use it in a sentence.

Definition in your own words	**Characteristics**
When settlers move to a region, they change it by bringing with them living things (like horses) and ideas (like music and religion).	• people starting farms • people putting up buildings and roads • people introducing plants and animals in a new area

colonization

NonCharacteristics	**Picture or Sentence**
• wilderness • any place untouched by humans • plants and animals that are native to the area	When people move into an area, they bring their plants, animals, ideas, and culture with them. This changes the area forever.

Now use the word map below to explore the meaning of the word *industrialization.* You may use your student text, a dictionary, and/or a thesaurus to complete each of the four sections.

Definition in your own words	**Characteristics**

industrialization

NonCharacteristics	**Picture or Sentence**

Make a word map of your own on a separate piece of paper for the word *suburbs.*

Core Concepts 4.3: Word Wise

Sentence Builder Complete the sentences using the information you learned in this section. Be sure to include terminal punctuation.

1. **Deforestation** is the result of _____

   _____

2. Air **pollution** occurs when _____

   _____

3. In an area with **biodiversity**, you would expect _____

   _____

4. A child with asthma who lives in an area with smog may suffer from

   spillover because _____

   _____

Sum It Up

Make Connections Use what you learned in this section to answer these questions.

1 Think about how land use has changed since the 1800s. How do you think the world's supply of nonrenewable resources has been affected by these changes?

_____

_____

_____

2 Imagine that a forest is being cut down to make room for new homes, farms, and roads. If a change in biodiversity takes place, is that an example of a spillover? Explain.

_____

_____

_____

3 How is using public transportation like buses and subways a way to conserve energy?

_____

_____

_____

4 Do you think building new suburbs helps or hurts the environment? Support your answer with evidence from the text or your personal experience.

_____

_____

_____

Core Concepts 5.1: Word Wise

Vocabulary Quiz Show Some quiz shows ask a question and expect the contestant to give the answer. In other shows, the contestant is given an answer and must supply the question. If the blank is in the question column, write the question that would result in the answer given. If the question is supplied, write the appropriate answer.

QUESTION	ANSWER
(1) _____	(1) incentive
(2) What describes the value of what you decide to give up when you make an economic choice?	(2) _____
(3) _____	(3) economics
(4) What do you call the amount of goods or services available for use?	(4) _____
(5) _____	(5) consumers
(6) What word describes the degree of desire for a good or a service?	(6) _____
(7) _____	(7) producers
(8) What is the term for having a limited quantity of resources to meet unlimited wants?	(8) _____

Core Concepts 5.2: Word Wise

Crossword Puzzle The clues describe key terms from this section. Fill in the numbered *Across* boxes with the correct key terms. Then, do the same with the *Down* clues.

Across	Down
1. an organized way for goods and services to be exchanged	5. a decline in economic growth for six or more months in a row
2. the money earned by selling goods and services	6. a general increase in prices over time
3. the act of a company concentrating on just a few goods or services	
4. the money left after subtracting the costs of doing business	

Name _____ Class _____ Date _____

Core Concepts 5.3: Word Wise

Words In Context For each question below, write an answer that shows your understanding of the boldfaced key term.

1 What makes a person's way of life important in a **traditional economy**?

_____

_____

_____

2 Who makes economic decisions in a **mixed economy** and why?

_____

_____

_____

3 How do new businesses benefit from the freedom of a **market economy**?

_____

_____

_____

4 How does a **command economy** differ from a market economy?

_____

_____

_____

Name _____ Class _____ Date _____

Core Concepts 5.4: Word Wise

Word Map Follow the model below to make a word map. The key term *developed country* is in the center oval. Write the definition in your own words at the upper left. In the upper right, list Characteristics, which means words or phrases that relate to the term. At the lower left list Noncharacteristics, which means words and phrases that would not be associated with it. In the lower right, draw a picture of the key term or use it in a sentence.

Definition in your own words	Characteristics
a nation with a strong economy and a high standard of living such as Japan	• United States, Japan, Australia, many European nations • people have access to a lot of goods and services • people have medical care, homes, and wages

developed country

Noncharacteristics	Picture or Sentence
• developing country—a nation with a less productive economy and low standard of living such as Haiti • people struggle to have the basic necessities of life (food, clean water, shelter, and medical care)	Developed countries' strong economies are responsible for the high standard of living their people. Developing countries want to create strong economies for this reason.

Now use the word map below to explore the meaning of the word *technology*. You may use your student text, a dictionary, and/or a thesaurus to complete each of the four sections.

Definition in your own words	Characteristics

technology

Noncharacteristics	Picture or Sentence

Make word maps of your own on a separate piece of paper for these words: *development, gross domestic product,* and *productivity.*

Name _____   Class _____   Date _____

Core Concepts 5.5: Word Wise

Sentence Builder Complete the sentences using the information you learned in this section. Include terminal punctuation.

(1) Grain is one example of an **export** from the United States because it is

_____

(2) You might **trade** your _____ for _____

_____

(3) Consumers benefit from **free trade** because _____

_____

(4) China **imports** _____ from _____

_____

(5) An example of a **tariff** is a _____

_____

(6) The purpose of a **trade barrier** is _____

_____

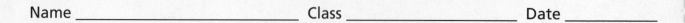

Name _____ Class _____ Date _____

Core Concepts 5.6: Word Wise

Word Bank Choose one word from the word bank to fill in each blank.
When you have finished, you will have a short summary of important ideas
from the section.

Word Bank

budget   credit
interest   invest
stocks   bonds
saving

You have options for using your money wisely. For example,

_____ funds in a bank, credit union, or other financial

institution ensures that you will have money for future use. You can take

some of that money and _____ it. Hopefully this will earn

you a profit. One way to do this is to buy _____, which are

certificates from a business or the government promising to pay back your

money plus additional money. Another way to do it is to purchase

_____, which give you shares of ownership in a company.

Of course, people also buy expensive things such as a car or a home

even though they do not have enough money to pay for it in full. To do this,

most people use _____. This means that they agree to pay

for their purchase over time. As they pay back the loan, they will also have

to pay _____. If this seems complex, don't worry. You can

create and stick to a money-management plan called a(n)

_____. It will help you to save more and to avoid borrowing

too much money.

Name _____ Class _____ Date _____

Sum It Up

Think About It Use what you learned in this section to answer these questions about Myra and the way she uses her money.

1. Your friend Myra is given $100. She wants to invest half of it so she can earn some more money. What do you think is the best way for her to do this? Why?

   _____

   _____

   _____

2. Myra plans to use the other $50 to buy a new pair of headphones. How might competition and specialization among headphone producers affect her choice?

   _____

   _____

   _____

3. Assume that Myra lives in a command economy. How do you think her headphone choices might be different from those in a market economy?

   _____

   _____

   _____

4. Now assume that Myra lives in a developing country. How might the supply and demand for $50 headphones be different than in a developed country?

   _____

   _____

   _____

Core Concepts 6.1: Word Wise

Word Bank Choose one word from the word bank to fill in each blank. When you have finished, you will have a short summary of important ideas from the section.

Word Bank

demographers	birth rate
infant mortality rate	death rate

There are many ways to investigate and measure an area's population

growth. For example, a country's _____, or the number of

live births per 1,000 people in a year, is an important measurement.

_____, the scientists who study human populations, often

compare this number to the _____, which is the number of

deaths per 1,000 people in a year.

When the birth rate is higher than the death rate, the population is

growing. But when the death rate is higher than the birth rate, the

population does not grow. Such slowdowns in population often take place

when people do not have enough food and clean water. A lack of food and

clean water often leads to a higher _____, which is the

number of infant deaths per 1,000 births.

Core Concepts 6.2: Word Wise

Words In Context For each question below, write an answer that shows your understanding of the boldfaced key term.

1. Think of what a typical U.S. town or city is like on a busy Saturday afternoon, when many people are running errands, shopping, and participating in other activities. Which parts of a town do you think have the highest and lowest **population density** on a typical Saturday?

    _____

    _____

    _____

    _____

2. How do you think changes in transportation over the past 100 years have changed **population distribution**?

    _____

    _____

    _____

    _____

Core Concepts 6.3: Word Wise

Word Map Follow the model below to make a word map. The key term *migration* is in the center oval. Write the definition in your own words at the upper left. In the upper right, list Characteristics, which means words or phrases that relate to the term. At the lower left list Noncharacteristics, which means words and phrases that would not be associated with it. In the lower right, draw a picture of the key term or use it in a sentence.

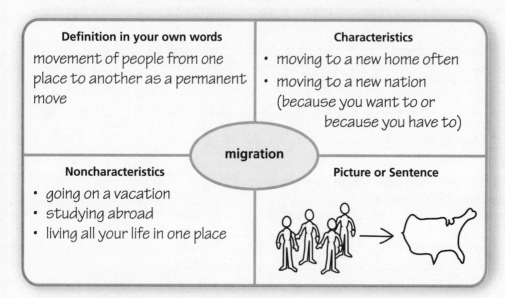

Definition in your own words
movement of people from one place to another as a permanent move

Characteristics
- moving to a new home often
- moving to a new nation (because you want to or because you have to)

migration

Noncharacteristics
- going on a vacation
- studying abroad
- living all your life in one place

Picture or Sentence

Now use the word map below to explore the meaning of the key term *push factor*. You may use your student text, a dictionary, and/or a thesaurus to complete each of the four sections.

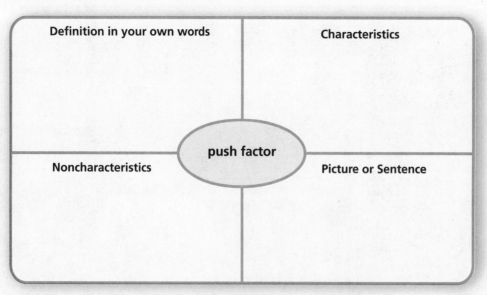

Definition in your own words

Characteristics

push factor

Noncharacteristics

Picture or Sentence

Make word maps of your own on a separate piece of paper for the following words: *emigrate, immigrate,* and *pull factor*.

Name _____   Class _____   Date _____

Core Concepts 6.4: Word Wise

Vocabulary Quiz Show Some quiz shows ask a question and expect the contestant to give the answer. In other shows, the contestant is given an answer and must supply the question. If the blank is in the question column, write the question that would result in the answer given. If the question is supplied, write the appropriate answer.

QUESTION	ANSWER
① What do you call a poor, overcrowded urban area?	① _____
② _____	② urbanization
③ What occurs when the population of a city begins to spread away from the center of the city?	③ _____
④ _____	④ rural
⑤ A city is what type of area?	⑤ _____

Sum It Up

Predict Imagine that you are a demographer. The mayor of a city that has recently experienced rapid population growth has asked you to investigate why his region is growing so quickly. Use what you learned in this section to predict three reasons for any city's growth.

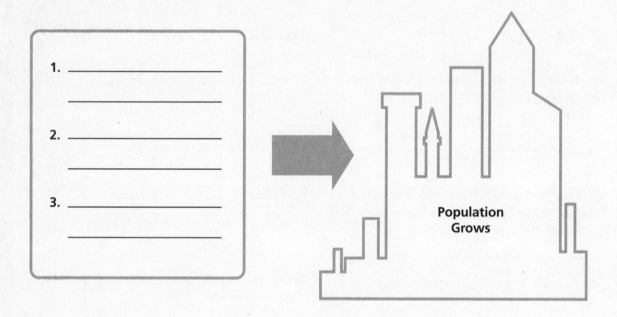

1. _____

   _____

2. _____

   _____

3. _____

   _____

Population Grows

Now imagine that the mayor of a city that has recently seen its population decrease has asked for your help. Use what you learned in this section to predict three reasons for any city's drop in population.

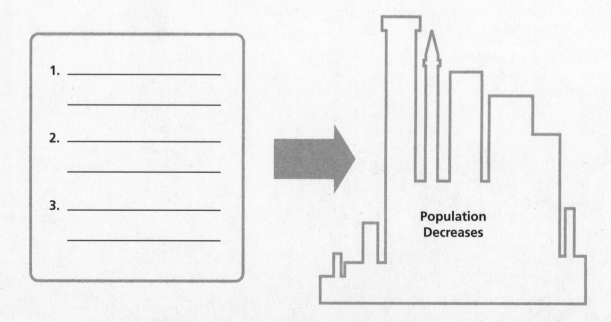

1. _____

   _____

2. _____

   _____

3. _____

   _____

Population Decreases

Name _____ Class _____ Date _____

Core Concepts 7.1: Word Wise

Sentence Builder Complete the sentences using the information you learned in this section. Include terminal punctuation.

(1) In modern American culture, one example of a **norm** is _____

_____

(2) Examples of **cultural traits** are language, _____

_____

(3) Human activities define the **cultural landscape** by _____

_____

(4) A nation's **culture** includes its _____

_____

(5) A **culture region** can extend beyond a nation's borders because _____

_____

Core Concepts 7.2: Word Wise

Vocabulary Quiz Show Some quiz shows ask a question and expect the contestant to give the answer. In other shows, the contestant is given an answer and must supply the question. If the blank is in the question column, write the question that would result in the answer given. If the question is supplied, write the appropriate answer.

QUESTION

ANSWER

(1) What is the basic unit of any society?

(1) _____

(2) _____

(2) nuclear family

(3) What word describes a human group that meets its basic needs in a shared culture?

(3) _____

(4) _____

(4) extended family

(5) What term describes people who share the same standard of living based on their economic status?

(5) _____

(6) _____

(6) social structure

Name _____ Class _____ Date _____

Core Concepts 7.3: Word Wise

Word Map Follow the model below to make a word map. The key term
communicate is in the center oval. Write the definition in your own words
at the upper left. In the upper right, list characteristics, which means words
or phrases that relate to the term. At the lower left list noncharacteristics,
which means words and phrases that would not be associated with it. In the
lower right, draw a picture of the key term or use it in a sentence.

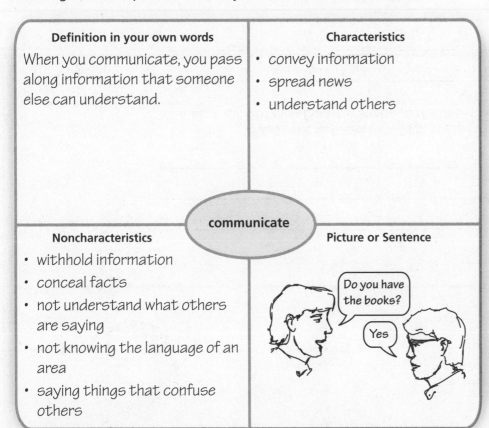

Now use the word map below to explore the meaning of the word
language. You may use your student text, a dictionary, and/or a thesaurus
to complete each of the four sections.

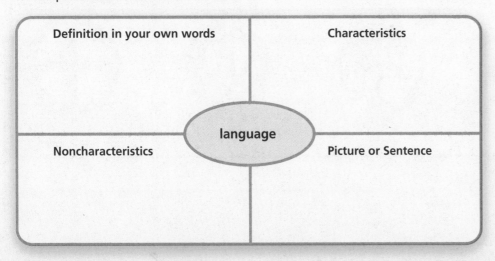

Core Concepts 7.4: Word Wise

Words In Context For each question below, write an answer that shows your understanding of the boldfaced key term.

(1) Why do many people value **religion**, and what do they hope to gain from it?

_____

_____

_____

(2) Which situation would test your **ethics**: learning how to drive a car or deciding whether or not to copy someone else's homework? Explain.

_____

_____

_____

Name _____   Class _____   Date _____

Core Concepts 7.5: Word Wise

Crossword Puzzle The clues describe key terms from this section. Fill in the numbered *Across* boxes with the correct key terms. Then, do the same with the *Down* clues.

Across	Down
1. an art form that uses sound	4. written works of art
2. an idea reflected in artwork that relates to the whole world	5. a person who designs buildings
3. the process of designing and constructing buildings	6. works of art that are seen instead of read or heard

Core Concepts 7.6: Word Wise

Sentence Builder Complete the sentences using the information you learned in this section. Include terminal punctuation.

(1) Ideas such as _____ and _____ spread

outward from a **cultural hearth** when _____

_____

(2) One example of **diversity** is _____

_____

(3) Traders were partially responsible for **cultural diffusion** because _____

_____

Name _____ Class _____ Date _____

Core Concepts 7.7: Word Wise

Word Bank Choose one word from the word bank to fill in each blank. When you have finished, you will have a short summary of important ideas from the section.

Word Bank

irrigate	science
technologies	standard of living

Throughout history, cultural development follows people's discoveries

about the natural world. New understandings in _____

helped ancient groups change from a life of hunting and gathering to

farming. For example, new _____ such as metalworking let

people create tools that helped them to clear land and to grow crops. When

people learned to _____ land, it increased the chances for

successful agriculture by making more land arable and providing some

protection against droughts.

As agriculture—and later industry—became central to world

economies, people were able to improve their _____ and

afford more goods and services.

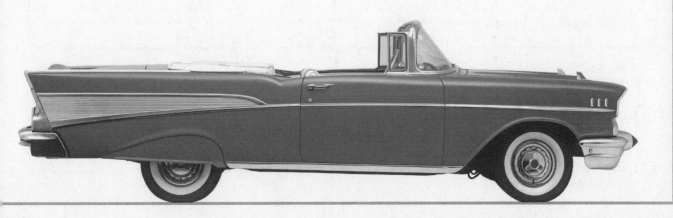

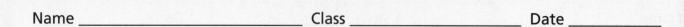

Name _____ Class _____ Date _____

Sum It Up

Draw and Label Imagine that you have been given the chance to create a
new town with new cultural elements. Draw a scene of everyday life in your
new town, representing and labeling all of the concepts listed in the key.

> **KEY**
>
> **A** = cultural trait   **B** = language   **C** = art   **D** = technology

Answer these questions about your town on a separate piece of paper:

1. Describe the technology you included. How does it affect daily life in
the town?

2. Describe diversity in the town. How does this diversity influence the
town's overall culture?

Core Concepts 8.1: Word Wise

Sentence Builder Complete the sentences using the information you learned in this section. Include terminal punctuation.

(1) Two goals of a **government** are _____

_____

(2) A **constitution** is a system _____

_____

(3) In a **limited government**, _____

_____

(4) In an **unlimited government**, _____

_____

(5) **Tyranny** can result in an abuse of power such as _____

_____

Core Concepts 8.2: Word Wise

Crossword Puzzle The clues describe key terms from this section. Fill in the numbered *Across* boxes with the correct key terms. Then, do the same with the *Down* clues.

Across	Down
1. In the political system called _____, the government owns all the property.	5. another name for a nation or country
2. One person or a small group holds all the power in a(n) _____ government.	6. A(n) _____ consists of several nations or territories and may be quite large.
3. In a(n) _____, the citizens have political power.	7. a country led by a king or a queen
4. A city and surrounding area that form an independent state is a(n) _____.	

Name _____ Class _____ Date _____

Core Concepts 8.3: Word Wise

Word Map Follow the model below to make a word map. The term *unitary system* is in the center oval. Write the definition in your own words at the upper left. In the upper right, list Characteristics, which means words or phrases that relate to the term. At the lower left list Noncharacteristics, which means words and phrases that would not be associated with it. In the lower right, draw a picture of the key term or use it in a sentence.

Definition in your own words	Characteristics
a central government that makes laws for the whole country	• single government • centralized government • most nations today
unitary system	
Noncharacteristics	Picture or Sentence
• federal system • divided government • confederal system • United States	A country with a unitary system has a very powerful central government.

Now use the word map below to explore the meaning of the term *federal system*. You may use your student text, a dictionary, and/or a thesaurus to complete each of the four sections.

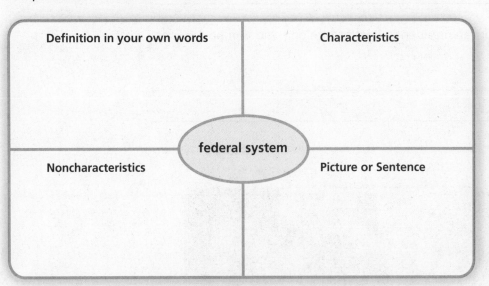

Definition in your own words	Characteristics
federal system	
Noncharacteristics	Picture or Sentence

Core Concepts 8.4: Word Wise

Words In Context For each question below, write an answer that shows your understanding of the boldfaced key term.

1 How is a **treaty** an example of international cooperation?

_____

_____

_____

2 How does **foreign policy** affect both the country that makes it and other countries?

_____

_____

_____

3 How might a nation's foreign policy protect its **sovereignty**?

_____

_____

_____

4 How are an American president's visits to foreign nations important for **diplomacy**?

_____

_____

_____

Name _____ Class _____ Date _____

Core Concepts 8.5: Word Wise

Word Bank Choose one word from the word bank to fill in each blank. When you have finished, you will have a short summary of important ideas from the section.

Word Bank

political party	civic life
citizens	civic participation
interest group	

   People born in the United States or who have completed the

naturalization process are U.S. _____. There are a number

of ways to take advantage of the privileges of citizenship. For example, you

may register to become a member of a _____ that reflects

your political views. Becoming involved with this group and other

organizations is a simple, effective way of participating in

_____. Voting, speaking out in meetings, signing petitions,

or simply staying informed are other kinds of _____.

If there is a certain issue about which you feel strongly, you may want to

join a related _____ dedicated to that particular cause.

Sum It Up

Predict Read each boldfaced statement. Think about what you read in this section. Then, consider the change given in the sentence starters. In each case you are making a logical prediction based on what you learned in this chapter. Include terminal punctuation.

1. **Country A is a representative democracy with a federal system of government.**

    If Country A switches to a unitary system of government, then _____

    _____

    _____

2. **Country B is made up of territory on one continent.**

    If Country B changes its foreign policy to become an overseas empire, then

    _____

    _____

3. **Country C has had the same constitution for 150 years.**

    If Country C's government becomes authoritarian, then _____

    _____

    _____

4. **Country D has a limited government made up of people from several political parties.**

    If Country D changes to unlimited government, then _____

    _____

    _____

5. **Country E has always encouraged the civic participation of its citizens.**

    If Country E's government becomes a tyranny, then _____

    _____

    _____

Name _____ Class _____ Date _____

Core Concepts 9.1: Word Wise

Crossword Puzzle The clues are definitions of key terms from this section.
Fill in the numbered *Across* boxes with the correct key terms. Then, do the
same with the *Down* clues.

Across	Down
1. a length of time that is important because of certain events or developments that occurred during that era	3. a person who studies, describes, and explains the past
2. a graphic organizer that shows events in the chronological order in which they happened	4. a list of events in the order in which they took place
	5. the time before humans invented writing

Core Concepts 9.2: Word Wise

Words In Context For each question below, write an answer that shows your understanding of the boldfaced key term.

(1) Why is an article written about a famous explorer considered a **secondary source**?

_____

_____

_____

(2) Why do museums collect and display **artifacts**?

_____

_____

_____

(3) When researching a topic, why must you be on guard against **bias**?

_____

_____

_____

(4) If you were doing a project about a famous battle, what **primary sources** might you use?

_____

_____

_____

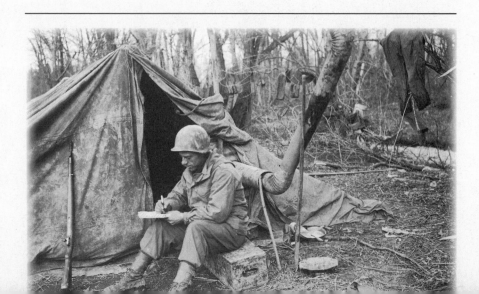

Name _____ Class _____ Date _____

Core Concepts 9.3: Word Wise

Word Bank Choose one word from the word bank to fill in each blank. When you have finished, you will have a short summary of important ideas from the section.

Word Bank
archaeology
anthropology
oral tradition

For centuries before people began to record information by writing,

history and culture was communicated to younger generations through

_____. By passing down information through songs and

storytelling, people were able to continue their traditions for hundreds

of years.

Today, people involved in the field of _____ study this

practice as well as other aspects of how different cultures developed. These

historians also depend on the findings of the people who work in

_____. Using evidence from artifacts, scientists in this field

determine how people behaved and what their culture was like.

Core Concepts 9.4: Word Wise

Word Map Follow the model below to make a word map. The key term *locate* is in the center oval. Write the definition in your own words at the upper left. In the upper right, list Characteristics, which means words or phrases that relate to the term. At the lower left list Noncharacteristics, which means words and phrases that would not be associated with it. In the lower right, draw a picture of the key term or use it in a sentence.

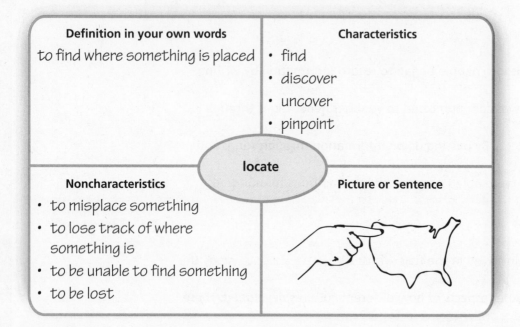

Definition in your own words
to find where something is placed

Characteristics
- find
- discover
- uncover
- pinpoint

locate

Noncharacteristics
- to misplace something
- to lose track of where something is
- to be unable to find something
- to be lost

Picture or Sentence

Now use the word map below to explore the meaning of the word *historical map*. You may use your student text, a dictionary, and/or a thesaurus to complete each of the four sections.

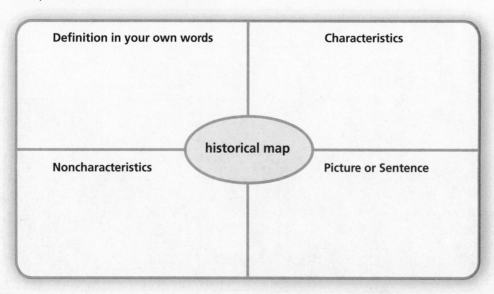

Definition in your own words

Characteristics

historical map

Noncharacteristics

Picture or Sentence

Name _____ Class _____ Date _____

Sum It Up

Be a History Detective Imagine that it has just been revealed that a famous American was actually a spy for another country. You are a historian collecting information for a documentary about this American's secret life. Explain how you would use each type of resource listed in the table's column headings. Include a specific example of each kind of resource. (You will need to use your imagination for this part.)

Primary Sources	Secondary Sources	Artifacts

Essential Question

How can you measure success?

Preview Before you begin this chapter, think about the Essential Question. Understanding how the Essential Question connects to your life will help you understand the chapter you are about to read.

Connect to Your Life

(1) Think of some ways to measure success in the categories shown in the table below. List at least one way in each column. For example, under family you could list getting along with your siblings.

Measures of Personal Success			
Family	• Friends	• School	• Other (Sports, Hobbies, Chores)

(2) Look at the table. Compare the ways to measure success. How are they alike? How do they differ?

_____

_____

_____

Connect to the Chapter

(3) Think about how to measure a country's success. For instance, a strong economy shows economic success. Preview the chapter's headings, photos, and graphics. In the table below, list one way to measure success in each category, and predict if the United States has achieved success in each. Include a reason: for example, if you think that the United States has too many social services that result in high taxes, it would show a lack of success.

Measures of National Success			
Economy	• Politics	• Social Services	• Environment

(4) Read the chapter. Then, circle your correct predictions.

Name _____ Class _____ Date _____

Connect to myStory: Finding Opportunity

1 Are you a "new American" who just recently arrived? Were you born in the United States? Were your parents? Do you know of any immigrants in your background?

_____

_____

_____

2 Have you ever visited another country? What things did you see there that were different from the United States? If you have never visited another country, write at least two things you would expect to be different in another nation.

_____

_____

_____

3 Suppose you were Vy's parents coming to live in a new country. What things would you be most worried about?

_____

_____

_____

4 What does Vy's life tell you about the opportunities immigrants have found in the United States?

_____

_____

_____

Word Wise

Words In Context For each question below, write an answer that shows your understanding of the boldfaced key term.

(1) When thousands of Europeans left their homes in the 1800s and 1900s, how did this effect **migration** to the United States?

_____

_____

_____

(2) Why is the **climate** for most of the continental United States considered **temperate**?

_____

_____

_____

(3) Where is **population density** at its lowest and its highest within the United States?

_____

_____

_____

(4) What is a **metropolitan area** like?

_____

_____

_____

Name _____ Class _____ Date _____

Take Notes

Map Skills Use the maps in your book to make a key and to label the Places
to Know on the outline map below.

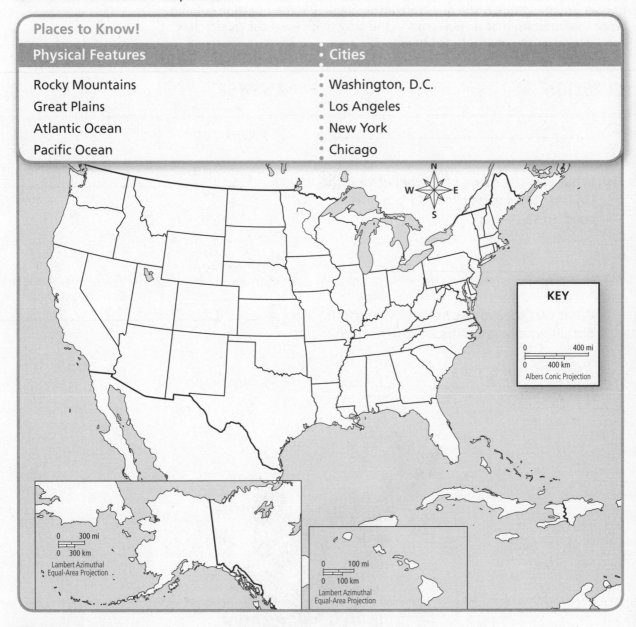

Places to Know!

Physical Features	Cities
Rocky Mountains	Washington, D.C.
Great Plains	Los Angeles
Atlantic Ocean	New York
Pacific Ocean	Chicago

KEY

0   400 mi

0   400 km

Albers Conic Projection

0   300 mi

0   300 km

Lambert Azimuthal
Equal-Area Projection

0   100 mi

0   100 km

Lambert Azimuthal
Equal-Area Projection

? Essential Question

How have natural resources created financial wealth
for the United States?

_____

_____

_____

Word Wise

Vocabulary Quiz Show Some quiz shows ask a question and expect the contestant to give the answer. In other shows, the contestant is given an answer and must supply the question. If the blank is in the question column, write the question that would result in the answer given. If the question is supplied, write the appropriate answer.

QUESTION

ANSWER

(1) _____

(1) cash crop

(2) What was the name of the belief that the United States must expand from one coast to the other?

(2) _____

(3) _____

(3) dissenter

(4) What was the name of the movement to obtain equality for African Americans?

(4) _____

(5) _____

(5) plantation

Name _____ Class _____ Date _____

Take Notes

Sequence In this section you read about the history of the United States. Complete the timeline below by writing the name of the event that occurred for each date or time period indicated.

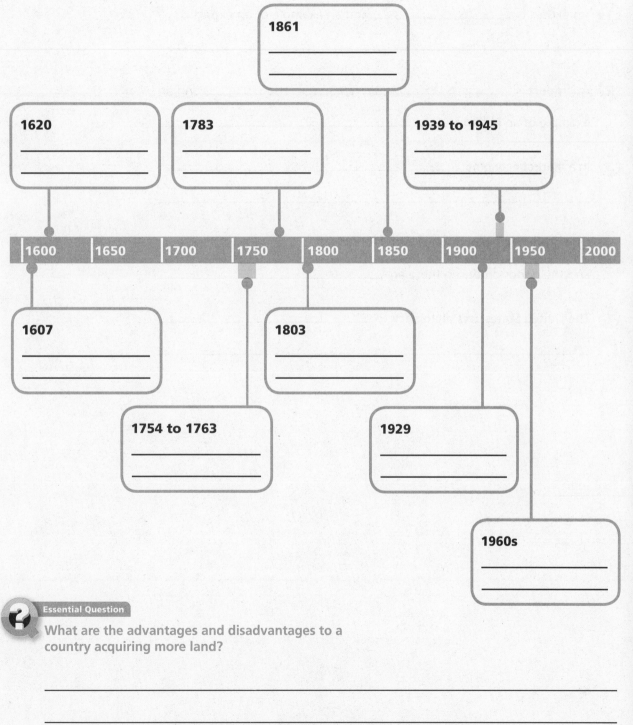

1861

_____

_____

1620

_____

_____

1783

_____

_____

1939 to 1945

_____

_____

| 1600 | 1650 | 1700 | 1750 | 1800 | 1850 | 1900 | 1950 | 2000 |

1607

_____

_____

1803

_____

_____

1754 to 1763

_____

_____

1929

_____

_____

1960s

_____

_____

Essential Question

What are the advantages and disadvantages to a country acquiring more land?

_____

_____

_____

Word Wise

Sentence Builder Complete the sentences using the information you learned in this section. Include terminal punctuation.

1. An **export** is _____, and an example of an **export** is

   _____

2. An **import** is _____, and an

   example of an **import** is _____

3. In a **market economy**, _____

   _____

4. One **economic region** in the United States is _____,

   and the goods produced there are _____

5. The United States uses **diplomacy** to _____

   _____

Name _____ Class _____ Date _____

Take Notes

Cause and Effect Use what you have learned about immigration to the United States to complete the graphic organizer below. Write one effect of immigration in each of the three categories.

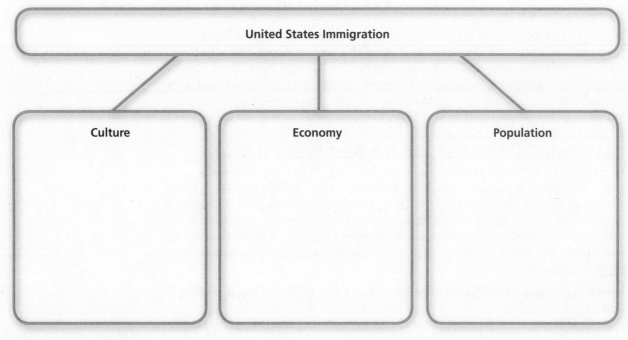

United States Immigration

Culture

Economy

Population

 **Essential Question**

Are there disadvantages to government involvement in events that take place around the world?

_____

_____

_____

Name _____ Class _____ Date _____

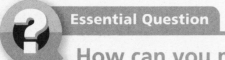

Essential Question Writer's Workshop

How can you measure success?

Prepare to Write

Throughout this chapter, you have explored the Essential Question in your text, journal, and On Assignment at myWorldGeography.com. Use what you've learned to write an essay measuring the success of the United States in one of the following categories: the economy, politics, social services, and the environment. Think about the amount of success achieved by the United States in that category and what caused the success or lack of success.

Workshop Skill: Understand the Four Types of Essays

First, decide what type of essay you want to write. There are four essay types: narrative, expository, research, and persuasive. A narrative essay tells a story and has a plot, characters, setting, and climax. An expository essay develops an argument about an idea, while a research essay contains information and evidence from a broad range of sources. A persuasive essay tries to get the reader to agree with a position by presenting evidence that supports the position.

Narrative Essay This essay is most like a story. It has characters, a setting, and a plot.
- Characters are the people that the story is about, and the setting is the time and place in which the story happens.
- A plot is the sequence of events that take place. Plots include conflict and lead up to a climax, which is the turning point of the story.

Expository Essay This essay has a main idea supported by evidence and examples.
- An introductory paragraph opens with a thesis sentence that states the main idea.
- The introduction is followed by body paragraphs. Each one discusses a point that supports the main idea. Evidence and examples are used to show that the supporting points are true.
- The conclusion sums up the essay by restating the thesis and supporting points.

Research Essay This essay has the same structure as an expository essay. The difference lies in the type of evidence used to prove supporting points.
- Evidence and examples should come from a broad range of reliable sources.
- Writers use quotations, footnotes, and a bibliography to show where they located evidence.

Persuasive Essay This essay is written when the author wants to convince readers to adopt an opinion or take action.
- The introduction tells why the topic is important. Then the thesis statement explains what the writer wants readers to think or do.
- In the body paragraphs, the writer uses strong arguments and evidence to prove the supporting points.
- The conclusion reviews the main points and urges the reader to adopt the opinion or take the action mentioned.

64

Identify Essay Types

Read the descriptions in the table below. In the column on the right, identify the essay described as narrative, expository, research, or persuasive.

Essay Description	Type
1. The essay tells a story about a nation in which three ethnic groups continually clash due to religious differences. The story ends when two of these groups make a truce.	_____
2. The essay states that access to medical care helps a developing nation's economy succeed by offering a more stable, healthy workforce. The essay includes graphs, charts, statistics, and quotations. Sources are listed in endnotes.	_____
3. The essay discusses how an aging population creates difficulties for a nation and explains three general problems that occur when there are more retirees than current workers.	_____
4. The essay urges businesses and environmentalists to compromise about natural resource development so that both sides can benefit. It cites examples of nations in which some natural resources have been used with minimal damage to the environment.	_____

Plan Your Essay

Use the following questions to help you make some decisions about your essay.

1. What do I want to say about the success or lack of success in the United States?

   _____

   _____

2. Do I want to tell a story, to explain an idea, present evidence, or persuade others?

   _____

   _____

3. Which essay type will best help me to accomplish my goal? _____

Draft Your Essay

Outline your essay. You will need an introductory paragraph, three body paragraphs, and a conclusion. Use the outline to write your essay. Then, proofread carefully.

Name _____ Class _____ Date _____

Is conflict unavoidable?

Preview Before you begin this chapter, think about the Essential Question. Understanding how the Essential Question connects to your life will help you understand the chapter you are about to read.

Connect to Your Life

1. What has caused conflicts in your family, school, community, or state? Name two recent conflicts.

_____

_____

2. Listed in the table below are three reasons for conflicts. Rate how apt each one is to cause conflict, with 1 being likely and 5 being unlikely. To help decide, you may want to consider the conflicts you named.

Reason for Conflict	How likely is it to cause conflict?				
Misunderstandings	1	2	3	4	5
Power struggles	1	2	3	4	5
Differences	1	2	3	4	5
Other: _____	1	2	3	4	5

Connect to the Chapter

3. Now think about sources of conflict in a country or region that can lead to tension (such as differences in economic opportunity). Preview the chapter by skimming the its headings, photographs, and graphics. In the web below, predict sources of conflict.

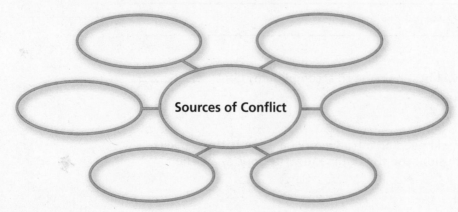

Sources of Conflict

4. After reading the chapter, return to this page and highlight your accurate predictions.

Name _____ Class _____ Date _____

Connect to myStory: Drawing on Heritage

① In Alyssa's story, you read about some of the traditional foods she enjoys sharing with her co-workers. Name at least three dishes they had at their "Country Food" luncheon.

② Now, think about foods that you enjoy that come from your own heritage. Write the name of at least two dishes and describe what is in them.

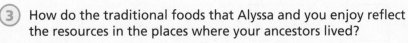

③ How do the traditional foods that Alyssa and you enjoy reflect the resources in the places where your ancestors lived?

_____

_____

_____

④ What does Alyssa's story tell you about the aboriginal peoples of Canada?

_____

_____

_____

Word Wise

Crossword Puzzle The clues describe key terms from this section. Fill in the numbered *Across* boxes with the correct key terms. Then, do the same with the *Down* clues.

Across	Down
1. a layer of soil that is frozen all year	4. any form of water, such as rain, snow, sleet, or hail, that falls from the sky to the ground
2. an ice mass formed from years of accumulated snow that may be moving very slowly	5. the area where warm and cold seawater combine
3. a treeless area lying above the tree line in an Arctic region that has permanently frozen subsoil	

Name _____ Class _____ Date _____

Take Notes

Map Skills Use the maps in your book to make a key and to label the Places to Know on the outline map below.

Places to Know!	
Physical Features	**Cities**
Canadian Cordillera	Ottawa
Canadian Shield	Montreal
Arctic Archipelago	Toronto
St. Lawrence River Valley	Calgary

KEY

0   400 mi

0   400 km

Lambert Azimuthal
Equal-Area Projection

Essential Question

What agreements reflect cooperation between the United States and Canada? How do they do so?

_____

_____

_____

Word Wise

Words In Context For each question below, write an answer that shows your understanding of the boldfaced key term.

(1) What was the **compromise** the British made in the Quebec Act?

_____

_____

_____

(2) Name two groups that are part of the **First Nations** and one group that is not.

_____

_____

_____

(3) Why was Canada originally called **New France,** and what happened to change its name?

_____

_____

_____

(4) Canada is a **dominion** of which nation?

_____

_____

_____

(5) How is a Canadian **province** similar to a state in the United States?

_____

_____

_____

Name _____ Class _____ Date _____

Take Notes

Sequence Use what you have read about Canada's history to complete this timeline. Identify the key event associated with each date on the timeline, then give a brief description of the event and its significance.

1775
_____
_____
_____

1608
_____
_____
_____

1867
_____
_____
_____

| 1600 | | | | 1700 | | | | 1800 | | | | 1900 | | | | 2000 |

1756–1763
_____
_____
_____
_____

1931
_____
_____
_____

1840
_____
_____
_____

Essential Question

How did Canada gain its independence from Britain?

_____
_____
_____

Word Wise

Word Map Follow the model below to make a word map. The key term *cultural mosaic* is in the center oval. Write the definition in your own words at the upper left. In the upper right, list Characteristics, which means words or phrases that relate to the term. At the lower left list Noncharacteristics, which means words and phrases that would not be associated with it. In the lower right, draw a picture of the key term or use it in a sentence.

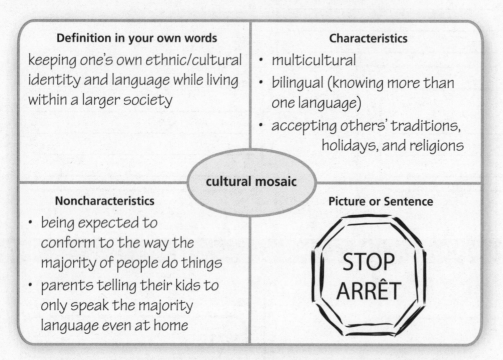

Definition in your own words
keeping one's own ethnic/cultural identity and language while living within a larger society

Characteristics
- multicultural
- bilingual (knowing more than one language)
- accepting others' traditions, holidays, and religions

cultural mosaic

Noncharacteristics
- being expected to conform to the way the majority of people do things
- parents telling their kids to only speak the majority language even at home

Picture or Sentence

STOP
ARRÊT

Now use the word map below to explore the meaning of the *constitutional monarchy*. You may use your student text, a dictionary, and/or a thesaurus to complete each of the four sections.

Definition in your own words

Characteristics

constitutional monarchy

Noncharacteristics

Picture or Sentence

Make a word map of your own on a separate piece of paper for the term *plural society*.

Name _____ Class _____ Date _____

Take Notes

Compare and Contrast Use the Venn diagram below to compare and contrast Canada and the United States. Include each nation's past and present relationship with Great Britain, the structure of their governments, their roles in the world, and how each nation has responded to racial diversity. For example, in the intersection where you write the elements that are the same, note that Canada and the United States both began as British colonies.

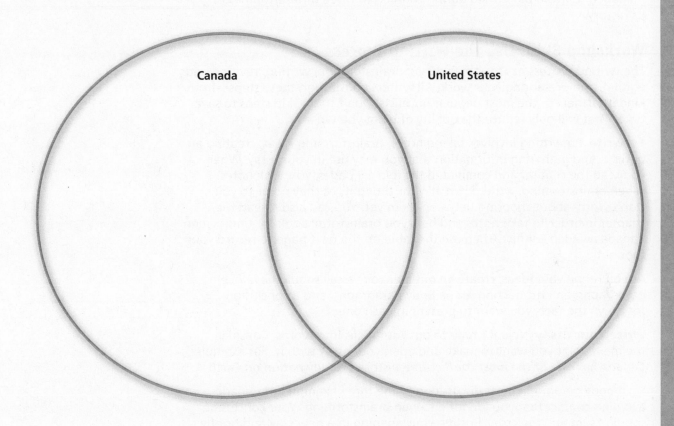

Canada   United States

Essential Question

Why is Canada known as a peacekeeping nation?

_____

_____

_____

Is conflict unavoidable?

Prepare to Write

Throughout this chapter, you have explored the Essential Question in your text, journal, and On Assignment at myWorldGeography.com. Use what you've learned to write an essay describing how the country of Canada managed to avoid bloodshed during conflicts in three different times in its history.

Workshop Skill: Use the Writing Process

The writing process has four main steps: brainstorming, writing, revising and editing, and presenting your work. All writers go through these steps—from kindergartners to the most popular novelists. Don't try to skip steps to save time! That will only reduce the quality of what you write.

Prewrite Prewriting involves taking notes, brainstorming ideas, creating an outline, and gathering information that you may use in your essay. When you read the chapter and completed the journal pages, you took notes. When brainstorming, write down all your thoughts as they occur to you. Don't worry about choosing between them yet. You can also reread the chapter in order to take notes and help you brainstorm. Look for times when Canada avoided conflict. Then use the table on the next page to record your thoughts.

As you refine your ideas, create an outline. Your essay should have five paragraphs: an introduction, three body paragraphs, and a conclusion. Jot down the facts you want to present in each one.

Write Your Essay Now it's time to put your ideas into words. Consider the main point you want to make and open your essay with it. For example: *Canada has one of the most conflict-free histories of any nation on Earth.*

Each body paragraph must discuss one of the three examples of Canada avoiding conflict that you identified when brainstorming. Your conclusion should "sum up" the essay. Restate your opening in a new way and briefly identify your three examples again.

Revise and Edit Your Essay Most people spend a lot of time revising. Why? They reread their essay aloud to find out if the sentences "flow." They rewrite to make sentences concise and organize ideas better. They check for grammar and spelling mistakes, remove sentence fragments, and fix run-on sentences. All of these things can trip up your readers so that they don't understand your essay. Take your time with this step. It may help to read your essay aloud to another person. He or she will tell you if something is confusing or unclear. Listen to what the person says.

Present Your Essay Rewrite your essay on a clean sheet of paper. Double space and include your name, date, and an essay title. Remember, this is your polished, final version. You want it to look and read its best!

Try Brainstorming

First, you may want to reread Section 2 of the chapter to refresh your memory. Then, answer these questions in order to pull together your thoughts for the essay:

When did Canada face conflict?	How was the conflict handled? (fighting or negotiation)	Was this a good example of conflict avoidance? (using negotiation instead of force)	
		YES	NO
		YES	NO
		YES	NO
		YES	NO
		YES	NO

Now consider the rows in which you answered YES in the third column. You are going to select three of these to write about.

Draft Your Essay

Use the information you brainstormed above to write a your essay on another paper. You should have five paragraphs: an introduction, three body paragraphs, and a conclusion. Follow the steps in the writing process to revise, edit, and present your essay.

Name _____ Class _____ Date _____

How much does geography shape a country?

Preview Before you begin this chapter, think about the Essential Question. Understanding how the Essential Question connects to your life will help you understand the chapter you are about to read.

Connect to Your Life

(1) Think about how the geographic elements in the table below have affected your life. Complete the table below with your ideas.

Personal Influence of Geographic Elements				
Parks, Lakes, Rivers	Local Weather	Local Crops	School Size	Recreational Activities

(2) In what ways can these elements affect each other? For example, in what way can cold weather affect the type of recreational activities in a region?

_____

_____

Connect to the Chapter

(3) Before you read the chapter, flip through every page and note the red headings, maps, and pictures. Think about ways that the influence of geography on families and communities applies to nations as well. In the table below, predict how geography has shaped Mexico.

Influences of Geographic Elements on a Country				
Physical Features	Climate	Natural Resources	Population	Culture

(4) After reading the chapter, return to this page. Were your predictions accurate? Why or why not?

_____

_____

Name _____ Class _____ Date _____

Connect to myStory: A Long Way From Home

1 Think about ways that your life is like Carolina's life. What challenges face your family every day? How does school play a role in your life? What are your hopes for the future?

_____

_____

2 Use this Venn diagram to compare your life with Carolina's life. Think about family challenges, school, and hopes for the future.

Your Life   **Both**   **Carolina's Life**

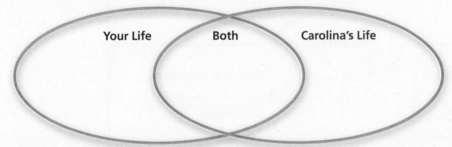

3 In this table, list the challenges Carolina faces as she tries to help her family meet its goals.

Daily Life	Making a Living	Getting an Education

4 How do you think these challenges are affecting the people of Mexico? Write your predictions below.

_____

_____

Name _____ Class _____ Date _____

Word Wise

Word Map Follow the model below to make a word map. The key term
sinkhole is in the center oval. Write the definition in your own words at
the upper left. In the upper right, list Characteristics, which means words or
phrases that relate to the term. At the lower left list Noncharacteristics,
which means words and phrases that would not be associated with it. In
the lower right, draw a picture of the key term or use it in a sentence.

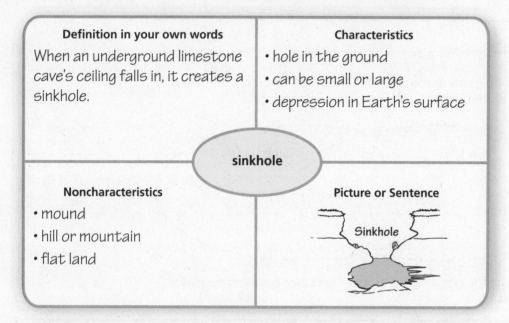

Definition in your own words	Characteristics
When an underground limestone cave's ceiling falls in, it creates a sinkhole.	• hole in the ground • can be small or large • depression in Earth's surface
Noncharacteristics	Picture or Sentence
• mound • hill or mountain • flat land	Sinkhole

sinkhole

Now use the word map below to explore the meaning of the word *altitude*.
You may use your student text, a dictionary, and/or a thesaurus to complete
each of the four sections.

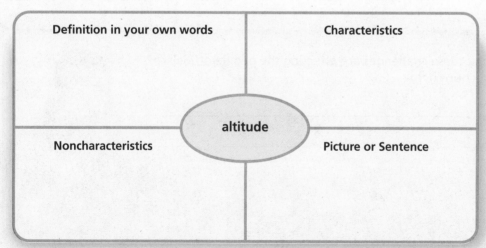

Definition in your own words	Characteristics
Noncharacteristics	Picture or Sentence

altitude

Make word maps of your own on a separate piece of paper for these key
terms: *irrigate* and *hydroelectric power*.

Name _____ Class _____ Date _____

Take Notes

Map Skills Use the maps in your book to make a key and to label the Places to Know on the outline map below.

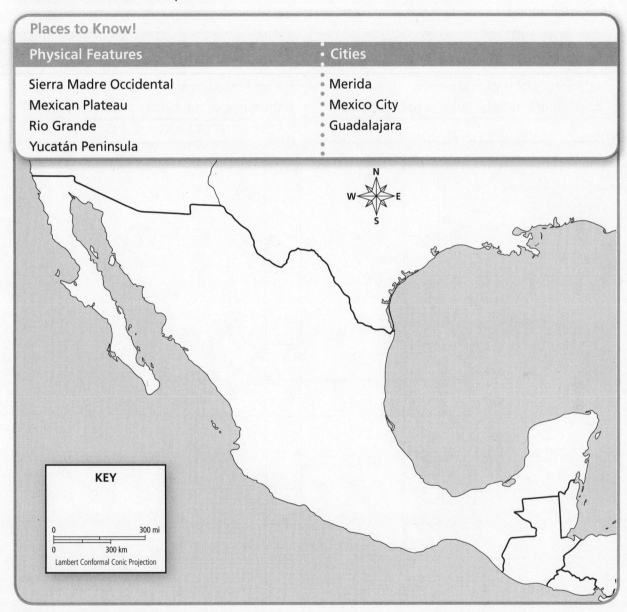

Places to Know!

Physical Features	Cities
Sierra Madre Occidental	• Merida
Mexican Plateau	• Mexico City
Rio Grande	• Guadalajara
Yucatán Peninsula	

KEY

0 ————— 300 mi
0 ——— 300 km
Lambert Conformal Conic Projection

Essential Question

What is one reason Mexico's population growth has concentrated near Mexico City?

_____

_____

_____

Word Wise

Crossword Puzzle The clues describe key terms from this section. Fill in the numbered *Across* boxes with the correct key terms. Then, do the same with the *Down* clues.

Across	Down
1. the study of stars and planets	3. a soldier-explorer
2. a channel made by humans to carry water	4. the name of the Mexican war of 1910–1917
	5. another name for corn

Name _____ Class _____ Date _____

Take Notes

Cause and Effect Use what you have learned about the history of Mexico to complete the table below. The first row has been completed for you.

Mexican History	
Event	Result
During the 1400s, the Aztec empire flourished.	The Aztec language, religion, and army spread throughout Mexico.
Hernan Cortés defeated the Aztec.	
In the 1700s, Spain sent new rulers to Mexico.	
In 1810, the Mexicans revolted against their leadership.	
Porfirio Díaz led Mexico.	
In 1910, the Mexicans revolted against their leadership.	

Essential Question

How did Mexico's geography and the struggle for resources affect the history of Mexico?

_____

_____

_____

Word Wise

Words In Context For each question below, write an answer that shows your understanding of the boldfaced key term.

1 Why did Mexican leaders adopt the **free market** economic system, and what happened to the Mexican economy when they did?

_____

_____

_____

2 For how many years did the **Institutional Revolutionary Party (PRI)** control the Mexican government, and why were the people frustrated by it?

_____

_____

_____

3 In what year did the **National Action Party (PAN)** first win the Mexican presidency, and what happened after that?

_____

_____

_____

4 How do **remittances** help to support both Mexican families and the national economy?

_____

_____

_____

Name _____ Class _____ Date _____

Take Notes

Main Ideas and Details In this section, you read about the modern
government, culture, and economy of Mexico. Each of the topics below
correspond to a heading in this section of the chapter. Use the graphic
organizer below to record the main ideas and details about these topics.

Topic: Governing Mexico

Main idea:

Details:

Topic: People and Culture

Main idea:

Details:

Topic: Mexico's Economy

Main idea:

Details:

Topic: Trade

Main idea:

Details:

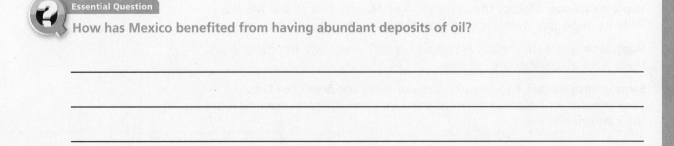

Essential Question

How has Mexico benefited from having abundant deposits of oil?

_____

_____

_____

Essential Question Writer's Workshop

How much does geography shape a country?

Prepare to Write

Throughout this chapter, you have explored the Essential Question in your text, journal, and On Assignment at myWorldGeography.com. Use what you've learned to write an essay describing how geography has shaped Mexico. You may include the following: the economy, politics, natural resources, and environment of the nation. In each category, consider how geography helped or hindered Mexico.

Workshop Skill: Write Body Paragraphs

Consider the main point you want to make in your essay. Phrase it as a thesis statement in your first (introduction) paragraph. For example, *The geographic variety of Mexico has both helped and hindered the nation.* In your introduction, support your thesis with three ideas.

In this lesson, you will learn how to write the body paragraphs of your essay—the three paragraphs in the middle of a five-paragraph essay. Each body paragraph should develop one of the ideas you listed in the introduction that supports your thesis statement. Each body paragraph takes the idea further by giving details or evidence.

Write a Topic Sentence Start each paragraph with a topic sentence. A topic sentence must clearly state the main idea of the body paragraph, connect that idea to the essay's thesis, and provide a transition from the previous paragraph. In this case, that paragraph was the introduction.

Support the Topic Sentence With Details and Facts After your topic sentence, you must explain and support your point with discussion and details. Discussion sentences connect and explain your main point and supporting details. Details provide the actual facts that prove that what you say is true.

End With a Concluding Sentence Finish your paragraph with one to two sentences that reflects your topic sentence and draws the discussion and details together. In the example below, the concluding sentence explains why few people live to the north or south of the Mexican Plateau. The final sentence also relates back to the topic sentence.

Here is a sample body paragraph:

Topic sentence *Most of the population of Mexico lives on the Mexican Plateau, although there are several problems with this region.*

Supporting detail *The soil in this area is soft, and some structures built there have actually sunk over time.*

Supporting detail *Two mountain chains flank the Mexican Plateau. They prevent air pollution from crowded Mexico City from escaping into the atmosphere.*

Supporting discussion *As a result, Mexico City has some of the worst smog in the world.*

Supporting detail *Fault lines also run through the Mexican Plateau, causing dangerous earthquakes.*

Concluding sentence *However, since it is almost as dry as a desert to the north of the Mexican Plateau and there are thick rain forests to the south, it is not surprising that so many people live on the Plateau.*

Write a Body Paragraph

Now write your own body paragraph for your essay. You may not have four supporting details or discussion; three will be sufficient.

Topic sentence _____

_____

Supporting (detail/discussion) _____

_____

Supporting (detail/discussion) _____

_____

Supporting (detail/discussion) _____

_____

Supporting (detail/discussion) _____

_____

Concluding sentence _____

_____

Draft Your Essay

Use the body paragraph above in your complete essay. Write it on your own paper. Be sure that each of your body paragraphs has a topic sentence, supporting details, and a concluding sentence.

Name _____ Class _____ Date _____

? Essential Question

Is it better to be independent or interdependent?

Preview Before you begin this chapter, think about the Essential Question. Understanding how the Essential Question connects to your life will help you understand the chapter you are about to read.

Connect to Your Life

(1) Think about ways in which you are independent and ways in which you rely upon others. For example, you may be independent in doing your homework, but you are interdependent on your parents for a home and food. In the chart below, list at least one advantage and one disadvantage of being independent and interdependent.

	Advantages	Disadvantages
Independent		
Interdependent		

(2) Think about situations in which you might prefer to be independent or interdependent. How do these situations differ?

_____

_____

Connect to the Chapter

(3) Before you read this chapter, flip through it. Look at the headings and pictures. In the Venn diagram below, predict ways in which the countries in Central America and the Caribbean are independent or interdependent.

Independent   Interdependent

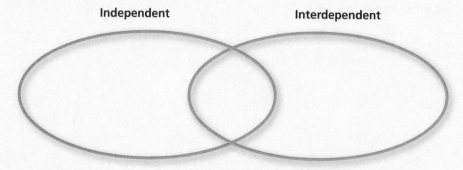

(4) After reading the chapter, return to this page. Circle your predictions that were correct.

Name _____ Class _____ Date _____

Connect to myStory:
Working for the Future

1. On the table below, list ways in which Luís is independent and interdependent.

Luís's Personal Independence and Interdependence		
	• Independence	• Interdependence
Family		
Friends		
School		

2. Compare what you wrote about Luís to your own life on the Essential Question Preview page. On the table above, underline or highlight similiarities.

3. Based on your preview of the chapter and what you read about Luís's life, make the following predictions:

Do you think the standard of living is adequate for those who live in the region's rural areas? Explain.

_____

_____

_____

What type of work does Luís do? Can this part of the economy be developed further?

_____

_____

_____

Word Wise

Word Bank Choose one word from the word bank to fill in each blank. When you have finished, you will have a short summary of important ideas from the section.

Word Bank

isthmus   biodiversity
tourism   deforestation
hurricanes

Central America is located on a(n) _____ that is rich in

_____. However, _____ has seriously

reduced the number of native plants and animals in the region.

Although Central America has its share of natural disasters such as

_____, many people vacation in Central American countries.

As a result, _____ contributes to the economies of these

nations. Plantations, or large commercial farms, are another important part

of the region's economy.

Name _____ Class _____ Date _____

Take Notes

Map Skills Use the maps in your book to make a key and to label the Places to Know on the outline map below.

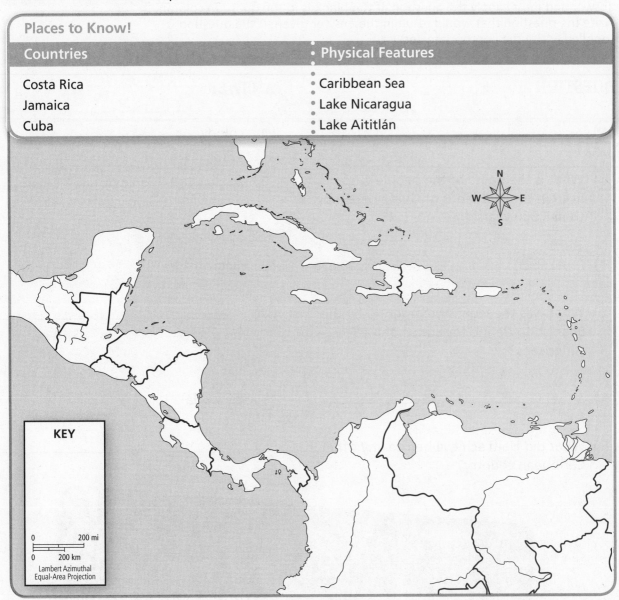

Places to Know!

Countries	Physical Features
Costa Rica	Caribbean Sea
Jamaica	Lake Nicaragua
Cuba	Lake Aititlán

KEY

0   200 mi
0   200 km
Lambert Azimuthal
Equal-Area Projection

Essential Question

How might the frequency of natural disasters affect a country's ability to be independent?

_____

_____

_____

Word Wise

Vocabulary Quiz Show Some quiz shows ask a question and expect the contestant to give the answer. In other shows, the contestant is given an answer and must supply the question. If the blank is in the question column, write the question that would result in the answer given. If the question is supplied, write the appropriate answer.

QUESTION	ANSWER
(1) _____	(1) colony
(2) What is the name of the people who lived in the highlands of Guatemala more than 3,000 years ago?	(2) _____
(3) _____	(3) dictatorship
(4) What was the legal system set up by the Spanish to define the status of Native Americans?	(4) _____
(5) _____	(5) hacienda
(6) What did Haiti achieve before any other Caribbean country?	(6) _____

Name _____   Class _____   Date _____

Take Notes

Cause and Effect In this section you read how Spanish colonists established
the encomienda system. Use the graphic organizer below to show the effects
of this system on the region's Native Americans, Africans, and Spaniards.

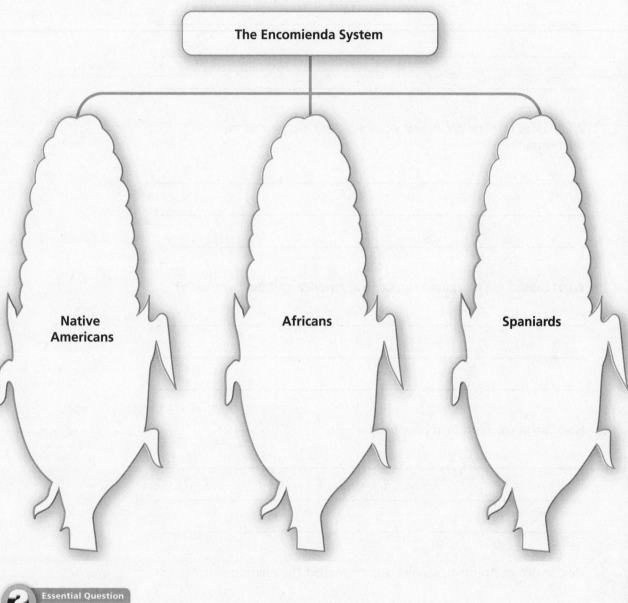

The Encomienda System

Native
Americans

Africans

Spaniards

Essential Question

Were the Spanish colonists independent or interdependent?

_____

_____

_____

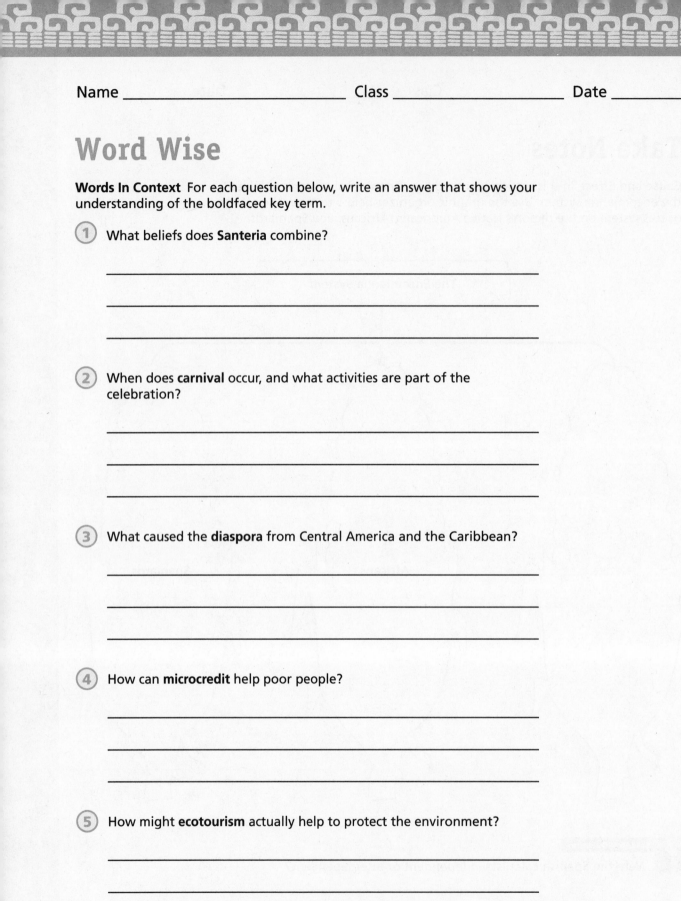

Name _____ Class _____ Date _____

Word Wise

Words In Context For each question below, write an answer that shows your understanding of the boldfaced key term.

1 What beliefs does **Santeria** combine?

_____

_____

_____

2 When does **carnival** occur, and what activities are part of the celebration?

_____

_____

_____

3 What caused the **diaspora** from Central America and the Caribbean?

_____

_____

_____

4 How can **microcredit** help poor people?

_____

_____

_____

5 How might **ecotourism** actually help to protect the environment?

_____

_____

_____

Name _____ Class _____ Date _____

Take Notes

Summarize Use the web below to summarize what you have learned about the governments and economies of present-day Central America and the Caribbean. For the top section, fill in information about the different governments in the area. For the bottom section, fill in information about the different economies in the region.

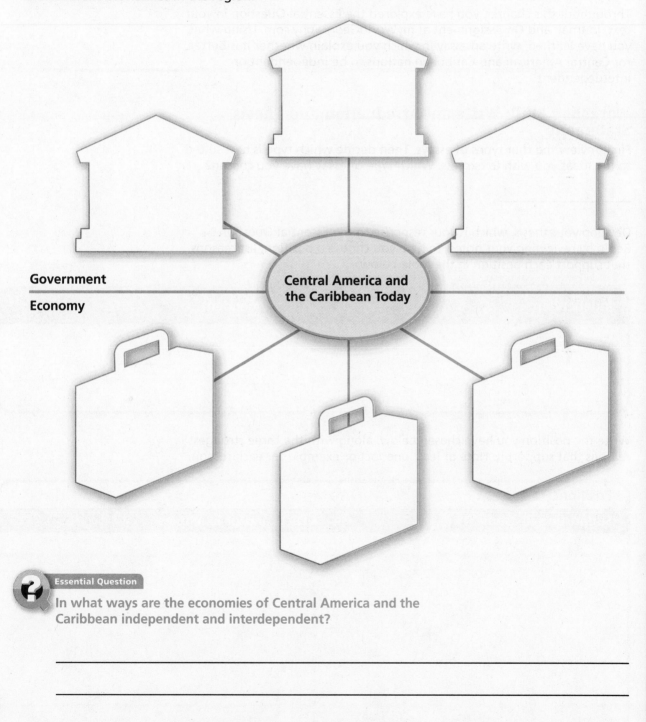

Government

Economy

Central America and the Caribbean Today

Essential Question

In what ways are the economies of Central America and the Caribbean independent and interdependent?

_____

_____

_____

Name _____ Class _____ Date _____

Is it better to be independent or interdependent?

Prepare to Write

Throughout this chapter, you have explored the Essential Question in your text, journal, and On Assignment at myWorldGeography.com. Using what you have learned, write an essay in which you explain whether it is better for Central American and Caribbean nations to be independent or interdependent.

Workshop Skill: Write an Introduction and Thesis Statement

First, review the four types of essays. Then decide which type is best suited to the ideas you wish to express. Which type of essay have you chosen?

_____

Develop your thesis, which is your response to the Essential Question. Begin by reviewing your notes. To help you choose a position, list reasons that support each position in the table below.

Independent	Interdependent

Write the position you have chosen below, along with the three strongest reasons that support it. Note at least one fact or example for each reason.

Position	
Supporting Reasons	**Facts and/or Examples**

Write Your Thesis Statement

Your thesis statement states your position and three reasons that support it. The thesis statement will be the last sentence(s) in your introductory paragraph. For example: *Independence is essential for Central American and Caribbean nations because*

_____, _____, and _____.

If your sentence is too long, place your reasons in a second sentence. For example: *Independence is essential for Central American and Caribbean countries. This is true because*

_____, _____, and _____.

Now write your thesis statement:

_____

Write Your Introduction

The first paragraph of an essay introduces the topic to the reader. An introduction has three parts:

1. A statement indicating what the essay is about.

Example *Independence and interdependence are characteristics that*

_____.

2. An indication of why the subject or issue is important.

Example *Understanding a particular nation's independence or*

interdependence is essential to understanding _____.

3. A thesis statement.

Write your introductory sentence: _____.

State the issue's importance: _____.

Write your thesis statement, including three supporting arguments:

_____

Draft Your Essay

Introduction: Rewrite your introductory paragraph on your own paper.
Body Paragraphs: Develop each argument to support your position in a separate paragraph. Include details and examples.
Conclusion: Summarize your arguments. When you have finished, proofread your essay.

Essential Question

Is conflict unavoidable?

Preview Before you begin this chapter, think about the Essential Question. Understanding how the Essential Question connects to your life will help you understand the chapter you are about to read.

Connect to Your Life

(1) What has caused conflicts in your family, school, community, or state? Name two recent conflicts.

_____

_____

(2) Listed in the table below are three reasons for conflicts. Rate how apt each one is to cause conflict, with 1 being likely and 5 being unlikely. To help decide, you may want to consider the conflicts you named.

Reason for Conflict	How likely is it to cause conflict?				
Misunderstandings	1	2	3	4	5
Power struggles	1	2	3	4	5
Differences	1	2	3	4	5
Other: _____	1	2	3	4	5

Connect to the Chapter

(3) Now think about sources of conflict in a country or region that can lead to tension (such as differences in economic opportunity). Preview the chapter by skimming the its headings, photographs, and graphics. In the web below, predict sources of conflict.

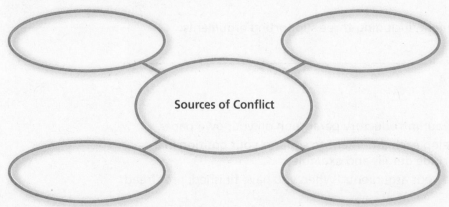

Sources of Conflict

(4) After you read the chapter, return to this page. Use a highlighter to mark your accurate predictions.

Name _____ Class _____ Date _____

Connect to myStory: Daniella's Coffee Run

(1) Describe at least two things that you can do to get along with other students.

_____

_____

_____

(2) Think of the things that Daniella does to get along with different people that she meets during her workday. Write your ideas in the appropriate row below.

People Daniella Meets	Things She Does to Get Along
Tourists	
Merchants	

(3) Do you think that Daniella's efforts to get along are helpful to her and to other people? Explain.

_____

_____

_____

_____

97

Name _____ Class _____ Date _____

Word Wise

Word Map Follow the model below to make a word map. The key term *ecosystem* is in the center oval. Write the definition in your own words at the upper left. In the upper right, list Characteristics, which means words or phrases that relate to the term. At the lower left list Noncharacteristics, which means words and phrases that would not be associated with it. In the lower right, draw a picture of the key term or use it in a sentence.

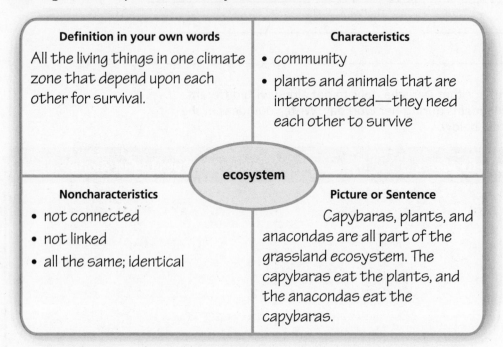

Definition in your own words
All the living things in one climate zone that depend upon each other for survival.

Characteristics
- community
- plants and animals that are interconnected—they need each other to survive

ecosystem

Noncharacteristics
- not connected
- not linked
- all the same; identical

Picture or Sentence
Capybaras, plants, and anacondas are all part of the grassland ecosystem. The capybaras eat the plants, and the anacondas eat the capybaras.

Now use the word map below to explore the meaning of the word *cordillera*. You may use your student text, a dictionary, and/or a thesaurus to complete each of the four sections.

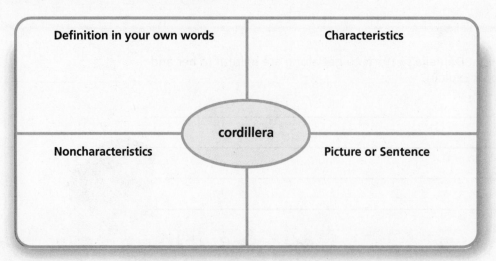

Definition in your own words

Characteristics

cordillera

Noncharacteristics

Picture or Sentence

Make word maps of your own on a separate piece of paper for these words: *Llanos* and *terraced farming*.

Name _____   Class _____   Date _____

Take Notes

Map Skills Use the maps in your book to make a key and to label the Places to Know on the outline map below.

Places to Know!	
Physical Features	**• Cities**
Cordillera Occidental	• Bogotá
Guiana Highlands	• Caracas
Orinoco River	• Georgetown
Llanos	• Cayenne

KEY

0   200 mi

0   200 km

Lambert Azimuthal
Equal-Area Projection

Essential Question

How might geography be a divisive force in the region?

_____

_____

_____

Word Wise

Words In Context For each question below, write an answer that shows your understanding of the boldfaced key term.

1. Why did Spanish invaders want to find **El Dorado**?

   _____

   _____

   _____

2. Once the area gained independence from Spain, what role did **caudillos** play in the new governments?

   _____

   _____

   _____

3. What are **paramilitaries** and how do they behave?

   _____

   _____

   _____

4. Why did Venezuela's government **nationalize** the oil industry?

   _____

   _____

   _____

5. What was the purpose of Pérez's **austerity measures** in Venezuela?

   _____

   _____

   _____

Name _____ Class _____ Date _____

Take Notes

Main Ideas and Details Use what you have read about the history of Caribbean South America to complete the graphic organizer below. Find the topic heading in the chapter. Write its main idea in your own words. Then give two details that support it.

Topic: Cultures Collide

Main Idea:

Details:

1.

2.

Topic: The Fight for Independence

Main Idea:

Details:

1.

2.

Topic: After Independence

Main Idea:

Details:

1.

2.

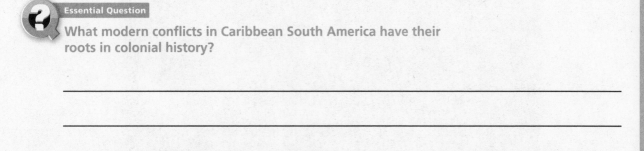

Essential Question

What modern conflicts in Caribbean South America have their roots in colonial history?

_____

_____

_____

Name _____ Class _____ Date _____

Word Wise

Vocabulary Quiz Show Some quiz shows ask a question and expect the
contestant to give the answer. In other shows, the contestant is given an
answer and must supply the question. If the blank is in the question column,
write the question that would result in the answer given. If the question is
supplied, write the appropriate answer.

QUESTION

① What do you call it when land sinks?

② _____

③ What word describes a person who rebels
against the government?

④ _____

ANSWER

① _____

② representative democracy

③ _____

④ Latin America

102

Name _____ Class _____ Date _____

Take Notes

Compare and Contrast Caribbean South America has great diversity. At the same time, the nations of the region have much in common. Fill in the table below to describe how parts of the region are alike and different.

	Similarities	Differences
Cultures		
Environmental issues		
Governments		

Essential Question

What issues fuel conflicts in Caribbean South America?

_____

_____

_____

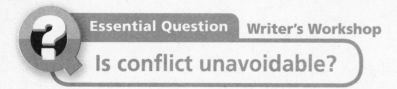

Essential Question Writer's Workshop

Is conflict unavoidable?

Prepare to Write

Throughout this chapter, you have explored the Essential Question in your text, journal, and On Assignment at myWorldGeography.com. Use what you've learned to write an essay on whether or not conflict is avoidable in Caribbean South America. Include information about tensions from racial and ethnic differences, the various governments, and religious and linguistic diversity. Also keep in mind how the region's history led to another source of conflict: differences in economic and social opportunity.

Workshop Skill: Write Body Paragraphs

Review the first steps of drafting an essay: writing a thesis statement and an introduction. Remember that your thesis statement presents the main point of your essay. Here's an example thesis statement: *Conflict in Caribbean South America may be avoidable due to efforts to reduce the causes of tension.*

Three body paragraphs should come between the introduction and conclusion in a five-paragraph essay. Each paragraph should develop one of the three ideas from your introduction. Each of the three paragraphs should contain: (1) a topic sentence; (2) details and evidence to help you make your point; and (3) a concluding sentence.

Write Your Topic Sentence Each body paragraph should begin with a topic sentence. A topic sentence serves two purposes: to state the main idea of the paragraph and to act as a transition from the paragraph before.

Sample Topic Sentence *Colonial oppression of Native Americans and slaves led to inequalities that still persist today.*

Support Your Topic Sentence Use details and explanations to support your topic sentence. Supporting details may include facts, quotations, examples, and other evidence. These supporting details help to prove that your ideas are correct. After each supporting detail, you may want to add a second sentence that discusses the idea.

Supporting Detail *There is a huge gap between rich and poor throughout the region.*

Supporting Discussion *A small minority has owned most of the land and wealth, which has led to civil conflict.*

Supporting Detail *In Columbia, paramilitary groups have fought to maintain privileges and power for the few, while rebel groups have fought for change for the many.*

Additional Supporting Detail *In Venezuela, the government has tried to close the gap by nationalizing the oil industry.*

End With a Concluding Sentence Wrap up each paragraph with a concluding sentence that ties together your supporting details.

Concluding Sentence *Efforts to correct imbalances have lead to gradual improvements, along with increased communication between opposing groups.*

Write a Body Paragraph Now write your own body paragraph for your essay. You may want to completely fill in the outline given below, or you may have a shorter paragraph.

Topic Sentence _____

_____

Supporting Detail _____

_____

Supporting Discussion _____

_____

Supporting Detail _____

_____

Supporting Discussion _____

_____

Supporting Detail _____

_____

Supporting Discussion _____

_____

Concluding Sentence _____

_____

Draft Your Essay

Use the body paragraph above in your complete essay. Write it on your own paper. Be sure that each of your body paragraphs has a topic sentence, supporting details, and a concluding sentence.

❓ Essential Question

What are the challenges of diversity?

Preview Before you begin this chapter, think about the Essential Question. Understanding how the Essential Question connects to your life will help you understand the chapter you are about to read.

Connect to Your Life

① Think about the wide range of differences in the likes and dislikes of a group of people. For example, you may like pizza prepared one way and a friend may like it with different toppings. Think about some general ways that in which people express their differences in taste. Fill in the table below with your ideas.

Categories	Clothing	Food	Music	Interests
Expressions of Different Taste				

② Do some differences in taste encourage or discourage interaction with other groups? Explain.

_____

_____

Connect to the Chapter

③ Preview the chapter by skimming the chapter's headings, photographs, and graphics. In the table below, predict the kind of challenges that diversity might present to the people of the Andes and the Pampas. An example is given in the linguistic category. Fill in a prediction of your own in each of the other columns.

Types of Diversity	Ethnic	Religious	Political	Linguistic
Challenges				When people do not share a language, they may have trouble communicating.

④ After you read the chapter, return to your predictions above. Did anything you learned about diversity in the Andes and Pampas surprise you? Explain.

_____

_____

Name _____ Class _____ Date _____

Connect to myStory:
Under the Rich Mountain

1 Think of high school students you know who have part-time jobs. How do their jobs differ from Omar's job?

_____

_____

2 In the diagram below, list details from Omar's story about the effects of Cerro Mountain on life in Bolivia.

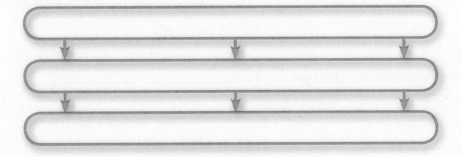

3 Think about Omar's story. What kinds of resources are mentioned? Write your predictions of how mining has affected this area.

_____

_____

Word Wise

Vocabulary Quiz Show Some quiz shows ask a question and expect the contestant to give the answer. In other shows, the contestant is given an answer and must supply the question. If the blank is in the question column, write the question that would result in the answer given. If the question is supplied, write the appropriate answer.

QUESTION	ANSWER
(1) What landform runs between the cordilleras?	(1) _____
(2) _____	(2) subducted
(3) What term describes how climate changes at different elevations?	(3) _____
(4) _____	(4) El Niño

Name _____ Class _____ Date _____

Take Notes

Map Skills Use the maps in your book to make a key and to label the Places to Know on the outline map below.

KEY

0 _____ 400 mi

0 _____ 400 km

Lambert Azimuthal
Equal-Area Projection

Places to Know!

Physical Features

Andes
Atacama Desert
Altiplano
Pampas
Rio de la Plata

Cities

Santiago
Buenos Aires
Lima

Essential Question

How does the geographic diversity of the region determine where people live?

_____

_____

_____

Word Wise

Word Bank Choose one word from the word bank to fill in each blank. When you have finished, you will have a short summary of important ideas from the section.

Word Bank

mercantilism   criollos
immunity   oligarchy
mestizos

The Incas were at the peak of their power when the Spaniards arrived

in 1532. Spanish weapons killed many of these people, and so did their lack

of _____ to European diseases. More and more Spaniards

settled in the Americas. Their children, born in the new land, were called

_____. The offspring of Spanish men and indigenous

women were known as _____.

Under the economic system of _____, the

colonists had to send their resources to Spain and also buy Spanish

products. After they achieved independence, landowners of Spanish

background set up a(n) _____ to control the nation.

Name _____ Class _____ Date _____

Take Notes

Cause and Effect Use what you have read about the history of the Andes and the Pampas to state what caused new people to come to the region and what effect they had on the region.

	Spanish Conquistadors	Immigrants in 1800s
Why did they come?		
What happened after they arrived?		

Essential Question

How has the history of the region contributed to its ethnic diversity?

_____

_____

_____

Word Wise

Words In Context For each question below, write an answer that shows your understanding of the boldfaced key term.

(1) Why is a **diversified economy** beneficial for the nations of the Andes and Pampas?

_____

_____

_____

(2) What is the purpose of the **MERCOSUR** trading bloc?

_____

_____

_____

(3) Why might the government of Bolivia want to improve its citizens' **literacy**?

_____

_____

_____

(4) When would a **referendum** be used in a democracy?

_____

_____

_____

(5) Why did the people of Chile vote to **amend** their constitution?

_____

_____

_____

Name _____ Class _____ Date _____

Take Notes

Summarize Use what you have read about the Andes and the Pampas today
to fill in the key ideas from this section of the chapter in the table below.

	Key Ideas
Cultures	
Environmental Problems	
Economies	
Governments	

? Essential Question

**In what ways have nations in the region tried
to diversify their economies?**

_____

_____

_____

What are the challenges of diversity?

Prepare to Write

Throughout this chapter, you have explored the Essential Question in your text, journal, and On Assignment at myWorldGeography.com. Use what you've learned to write an essay describing the challenges that diversity has caused in the Andes and the Pampas.

Workshop Skill: Write a Conclusion

Review how to draft an essay. Drafting requires writing a thesis statement, an introduction, three body paragraphs, and a conclusion. The conclusion wraps up your essay and brings everything together.

Writing a strong conclusion requires thought and effort. Remember, it is the last impression that your essay makes on your readers.

Preparing to Write Your Conclusion Before you write your conclusion, reread your essay. Think about your thesis, including the main ideas and details that support it. What new questions spring to mind? What related topic might you want to investigate at another time? Does the topic of diversity affect you personally? After you reread, brainstorm some responses to your new questions.

Use a Checklist When you're ready to write your conclusion, do so in an organized way. Follow a checklist like the one below. As you complete each task, check it off your list.

_____ Restate your thesis to remind the reader of the whole point of your essay.

_____ Summarize the most important ideas that support your thesis.

_____ Include a few sentences that add something new to your topic.

_____ Explain the importance of your topic and suggest its deeper meaning.

What Makes a Strong Conclusion? A strong conclusion should tie together the different strands of your essay. It should give your reader the feeling that everything adds up and makes sense. At the same time, your conclusion should be interesting, thought-provoking, and unique.

Sample Conclusion Here are some sample sentences that could be used to form a cohesive conclusion:

- Restatement of the Thesis *The region's mountains and grasslands shaped its history and led to great diversity.*

- Summary of an Important Idea *The gold and silver of the highlands attracted the conquistadors, who were followed by colonists and other immigrants.*

- A New Idea *If the region had not been so rich in silver and gold, its history might have been very different.*

- Why This Topic Is Important *Learning about the diversity of the region helps us to understand the problems the people in this region face today.*

Write Your Conclusion

Now write your own concluding paragraph for your essay.

Restatement of the Thesis _____

_____

_____

Summary of One Important Idea _____

_____

Summary of Another Important Idea _____

_____

Summary of One Important Idea _____

_____

A New Idea _____

_____

Why This Topic Is Important _____

_____

_____

Draft Your Essay

Use the concluding paragraph above in your completed essay. Write your essay on another sheet of paper.

? Essential Question

Who should benefit from a country's resources?

Preview Before you begin this chapter, think about the Essential Question. Understanding how the Essential Question connects to your life will help you understand the chapter you are about to read.

Connect to Your Life

1. How do you and your friends share? Think about sharing a bag of hard candies. What are the positives and negatives of different ways of sharing? List your ideas in the table below.

Different Ways to Share

Sharing/ Strategy	Equal portion for all	Biggest appetite gets more	More for those who pay more	Other
Pros				
Cons				

2. Why do people disagree about which sharing method is the best?

_____

_____

Connect to the Chapter

3. Now think about different ways that a country's resources might be distributed among citizens. For example, poor citizens might not benefit from a country's oil reserves. Preview the chapter by skimming the headings, photographs and illustrations.

4. Read the chapter. Think of how groups in Brazil have shared resources during its history in the ways shown in the table below. Write yes or no in the first row. For those columns in which the answer is yes, write the name of the group that used it in the second row.

Ways to Divide Resources in the Real World

Sharing/ Strategy	Shares are based on need.	Rich/powerful people take more than others.	Everybody fights.
Ever used in Brazil?			
Name (if yes)			

Name _____ Class _____ Date _____

Connect to myStory: Vinicius's Game Plan

(1) Do you think that teenagers should set goals for the future? Why or why not?

_____

_____

_____

(2) What is Vinicius doing to reach his goals? What obstacles, or problems, does he face?

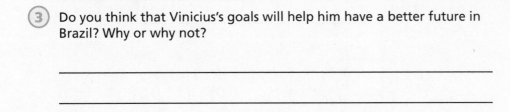

Goal 1: Become a professional soccer player (Plan A)
Things he is doing
Obstacles
Goal 2: Go to the university (Plan B)
Things he is doing
Obstacles

(3) Do you think that Vinicius's goals will help him have a better future in Brazil? Why or why not?

_____

_____

_____

_____

Word Wise

Crossword Puzzle The clues describe key terms from this section. Fill in the numbered *Across* boxes with the correct key terms. Then, do the same with the *Down* clues.

Across	Down
1. the topmost level of a rain forest	3. the land area that drains into the Amazon River
2. The Cerrado in the Brazilian Highlands is a vast _____.	4. a Brazilian slum

Name _____ Class _____ Date _____

Take Notes

Map Skills Use the maps in your book to make a key and to label the Places to Know on the outline map below.

Places to Know!	
Physical Features	**Cities**
Amazon River	São Paulo
Pantanal	Rio de Janeiro
Cerrado	
Guiana Highlands	

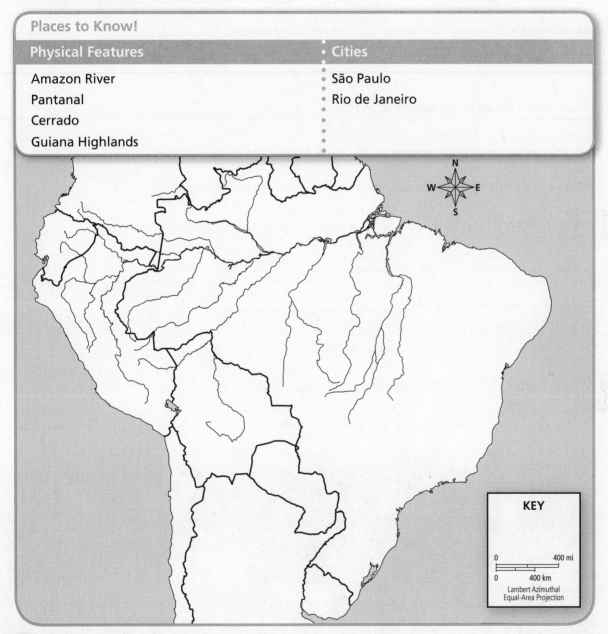

KEY

0   400 mi

0   400 km

Lambert Azimuthal
Equal-Area Projection

Essential Question

Where are some of Brazil's resources located? Explain.

_____

_____

_____

Name _____ Class _____ Date _____

Word Wise

Sentence Builder Complete the sentences using the information you learned in this section. Include terminal punctuation.

① **Brazilwood** is different from other kinds of wood because _____

_____

② The main feature of an **export economy** is _____

_____

③ **"Boom and bust" cycles** in an economy are the opposite of "steady and

even" cycles because _____

_____

④ An **abolitionist** is interested in _____

_____

⑤ When leaders worry about a **coup**, they fear _____

_____

Name _____ Class _____ Date _____

Take Notes

Sequence Use what you have read about the history of Brazil to complete the table below by filling in the missing date or event in each row.

Date	Important Events in Brazilian History
1494	The Treaty of Tordesillas gives Portugal colonization rights to Brazil.
1500	
	Portugal's royal family flees to Brazil.
1822	Brazil becomes an empire under Pedro I.
1888	
	Brazil becomes an independent republic.
	Dictator Getúlio Vargas overthrows the government.

Essential Question

Did the export of sugar and other valuable resources from Brazil benefit all the people in the colony? Explain.

_____

_____

_____

Word Wise

Vocabulary Quiz Show Some quiz shows ask a question and expect the contestant to give the answer. In other shows, the contestant is given an answer and must supply the question. If the blank is in the question column, write the question that would result in the answer given. If the question is supplied, write the appropriate answer.

QUESTION	ANSWER
(1) What do you call the deliberate designing of a city?	**(1)** _____
(2) _____	**(2)** ethanol
(3) What is the financial system in which the government does *not* set prices?	**(3)** _____
(4) _____	**(4)** social services

Name _____ Class _____ Date _____

Take Notes

Summarize Use what you have read about Brazil today to complete the table below. Under each heading, write at least two important ideas or details that sum up what that subsection is about.

A Rich Culture

1.

2.

Environmental Issues

1.

2.

A Growing Economy

1.

2.

Government for the People

1.

2.

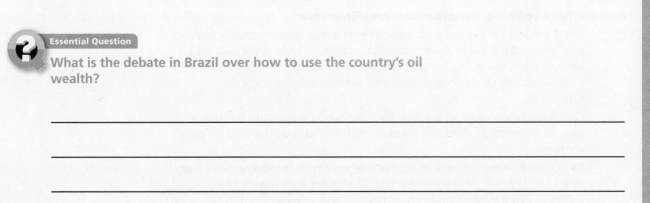

Essential Question

What is the debate in Brazil over how to use the country's oil wealth?

_____

_____

_____

Essential Question Writer's Workshop

Who should benefit from a country's resources?

Prepare to Write

Throughout this chapter, you have explored the Essential Question in your text, journal, and On Assignment at myWorldGeography.com. Use what you've learned to write an essay about who has benefited from Brazil's resources—and whether the division of resources is fair. Include information about the resources of the Amazon basin, the country's minerals, Brazil's boom and bust cycles, and the country's early economies based on sugar and coffee. You may want to add how the Portuguese legacy has affected the division of resources.

Workshop Skill: Revise Your Essay

Revising involves carefully reading over a draft of your essay to make it better. Revising comes *after* the first two steps of the writing process: (1) prewriting, and (2) drafting, when you develop and write your thesis statement, an introduction, at least three body paragraphs, and a conclusion.

In this lesson, you will learn more about revising. During this step, you will look closely at each part of your essay and at the paragraphs that make up each part. You will also focus on the individual sentences and words.

Improve Each Part of Your Essay

Use this checklist to revise your essay. As you complete each task, check it off.

_____ **The introduction** is the first impression you make on your readers. It should be clear and interesting. Your thesis statement should not be too general or too specific.

_____ **Each paragraph in the body** of your essay should have a main idea and several supporting details. Each paragraph should be logical and easy to follow.

_____ **The transitions** from one paragraph to the next should make sense.

_____ **The conclusion** is the final impression you make on your readers. It should be clear and interesting. It should be based on information from your essay.

Inspect Your Spelling, Punctuation, and Grammar

_____ **Read aloud** to make sure that each sentence is grammatically correct and interesting. Every complete sentence must have a subject and a verb. Within the essay, sentences should be varied. An essay should include simple sentences, compound sentences, and complex sentences.

_____ **Check each sentence** to be sure the first word is capitalized. Use a period, a question mark, or an exclamation mark at the end of each sentence.

_____ **Check each word** to be sure that is spelled correctly. Use a dictionary or a spell checker. Make certain that the verbs agree with the subjects. Capitalize the names of people and places.

Use Proofreading Marks

Proofreading Marks

C̲̲ capitalize	⊙· period
¶ start new paragraph	∧ insert a comma
ro ∧c k insert	ℓ delete

Here is a sample of a short paragraph that has been proofread. Changes have also been made to increase sentence variety.

¶ The mountins and forests of brazil hold amazing resources The forests produce fruits nuts, rubber, pam oil an timber. brazil has great minral wealth. There is iron or, bauxite, and gold, Portuguese traders set up an expart economy to profit from these resources.

Practice Revision

Revise the following paragraph. Use proofreading marks to show errors in capitalization, spelling, and end punctuation. Then, on the lines below, combine the two underlined sentences to improve sentence length and variety.

Portugal profited grately from the resources of brazil. First, they set up

trading posts They began exporting brazilwood. It was used for dye. They

added sugar, coffe, gold, and diamonds to their exports the native peoples

and the African slaves suffered under this unair system.

_____

_____

Revise Your Essay

Use the checklists given in this workshop and proofreading marks to revise your own essay. Then, rewrite your final draft on a new piece of paper.

Name _____ Class _____ Date _____

? Essential Question

What are the challenges of diversity?

Preview Before you begin this chapter, think about the Essential Question. Understanding how the Essential Question connects to your life will help you understand the chapter you are about to read.

Connect to Your Life

(1) Think of a time when you learned about another culture. Name the other culture and tell at least one way in which it differed from yours.

_____

_____

(2) Think about some general ways that in which people express their differences in taste. Fill in the table below with your ideas.

Categories	Clothing	Food	Music	Interests
Expressions of Different Taste				

Connect to the Chapter

(3) Preview the chapter. Skim the headings, photos, and graphics. In the table below, predict the challenges that diversity presented to the people living in ancient and medieval Europe. One example is given in the table.

Type of Diversity	Ethnic	Religious	Political	Linguistic
Challenges			People with different values have different political viewpoints. The values and political ides may actually be exact opposites.	

(4) After reading the chapter, put a check mark next to your ideas that turned out to be correct.

Name _____ Class _____ Date _____

Connect to myStory: Alexander the Great: A Prophecy Fulfilled

1 List the major events in your life up to now. You should write at least three.

_____

_____

_____

2 List the major events of Alexander's life in the boxes of the chart.

The Life of Alexander the Great

Growing Up   **Fighting Persia**   **Building an Empire**

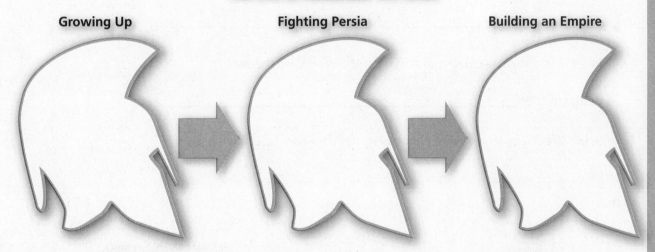

3 Look at the Growing Up box above. How do your life events differ from Alexander's early life events?

_____

_____

_____

4 What might be the challenges of ruling an empire as big and diverse as the one Alexander the Great conquered?

_____

_____

_____

_____

Word Wise

Sentence Builder Complete the sentences using the information you learned in this section. Include terminal punctuation.

(1) Greece is considered a **cultural hearth** because _____

_____

(2) Greek scholars started a branch of study called **philosophy** which

_____

(3) Two of the most famous Greek **city-states** were _____

_____

(4) In Athens, the male citizens took part in the world's first **direct**

democracy by _____

(5) Some Greek city-states were **oligarchies**, which means _____

_____

Name _____ Class _____ Date _____

Take Notes

Map Skills Use the maps in *all* sections of this chapter to make a key and to label the Places to Know on the outline map below. Remember, in addition to this section, you will need to refer to Sections 2 through 4.

Places to Know!

Physical Features	Countries/Empires	City-States and Cities
Aegean Sea	Spain	Athens
Crete	Italy	Sparta
Peloponnesian Peninsula	Holy Roman Empire	Constantinople
Mediterranean Sea	France	Rome
Balkan Peninsula		Venice
Black Sea		

KEY

0 _____ 400 mi

0 _____ 400 km

Lambert Conformal Conic Projection

Essential Question

How did the diversity of Alexander the Great's Empire affect Greek culture?

_____

_____

_____

Word Wise

Word Map Follow the model below to make a word map. The key term *patrician* is in the center oval. Write the definition in your own words at the upper left. In the upper right, list Characteristics, which means words or phrases that relate to the term. At the lower left list Noncharacteristics, which means words and phrases that would not be associated with it. In the lower right, draw a picture of the key term or use it in a sentence.

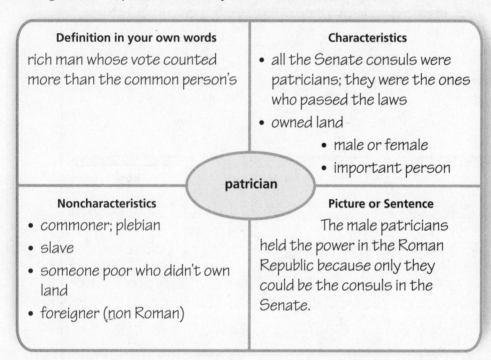

Definition in your own words

rich man whose vote counted more than the common person's

Characteristics

- all the Senate consuls were patricians; they were the ones who passed the laws
- owned land
  - male or female
  - important person

patrician

Noncharacteristics

- commoner; plebian
- slave
- someone poor who didn't own land
- foreigner (non Roman)

Picture or Sentence

The male patricians held the power in the Roman Republic because only they could be the consuls in the Senate.

Now use the word map below to explore the meaning of the word *representative democracy*. You may use your student text, a dictionary, and/or a thesaurus to complete each of the four sections.

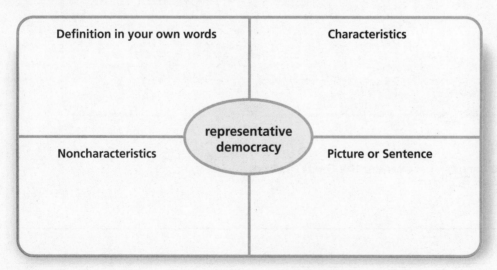

Definition in your own words

Characteristics

representative democracy

Noncharacteristics

Picture or Sentence

Make word maps of your own on a separate piece of paper for these key terms: *Pax Romana* and *aqueduct*.

Name _____ Class _____ Date _____

Take Notes

Sequence Record major events from the history of Ancient Rome on the timeline below. Check the section to be sure you are putting the events in chronological order.

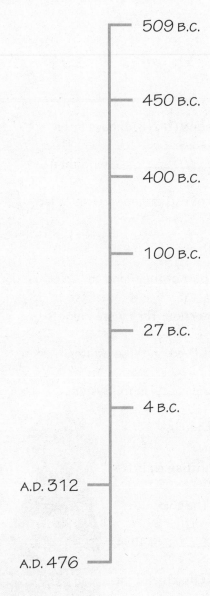

509 B.C.

450 B.C.

400 B.C.

100 B.C.

27 B.C.

4 B.C.

A.D. 312

A.D. 476

Essential Question

How did the Romans use citizenship to unify a diverse empire?

_____

_____

_____

131

Word Wise

Word Bank Choose one word from the word bank to fill in each blank. When you have finished, you will have a short summary of important ideas from the section.

Word Bank

Schism   lords
vassals   feudalism
manorialism

In Western Europe, a ruler named Charlemagne (742–814) gave large

pieces of land as estates to nobles called _____, who then

owed him services. This was the start of a system of exchanged services called

_____.

The nobles who received estates then gave part of their land to

_____ in exchange for their protection. They were knights

that gave military support to the nobles. Peasants lived on these estates

under the economic system called _____. In this system,

peasants worked the land for the nobles who owned it.

Meanwhile, in the Byzantine empire, the Christian church

developed differently from the Church in Rome. The two

churches split apart in the Great _____ of 1054.

After the division, there was the Roman Catholic Church and the

Greek Orthodox Church.

Name _____ Class _____ Date _____

Take Notes

Summarize Use the information in your textbook to complete this graphic organizer. In the top three boxes, record details about the roles that the king, the lords, and the vassals played in feudalism. Then in the bottom box, write a few sentences summarizing how the system of feudalism worked.

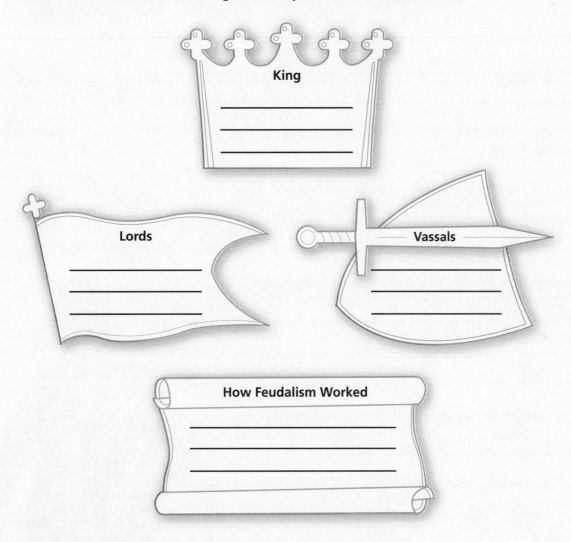

King
_____
_____
_____

Lords
_____
_____
_____

Vassals
_____
_____
_____

How Feudalism Worked
_____
_____
_____

Essential Question

How did cultural differences between the East and the West affect the Christian church?

_____

_____

_____

Word Wise

Words In Context For each question below, write an answer that shows your understanding of the boldfaced key term.

(1) Why did the craftspeople form **guilds**?

_____

_____

_____

(2) What did the Catholic Church hope that the **Crusades** would accomplish?

_____

_____

_____

(3) Who started the **Reconquista**, and what was its purpose?

_____

_____

_____

(4) How did the **Magna Carta** affect English government?

_____

_____

_____

Name _____ Class _____ Date _____

Take Notes

Cause and Effect Use this cause-and-effect graphic organizer to record information about the Crusades and the decline of feudalism.

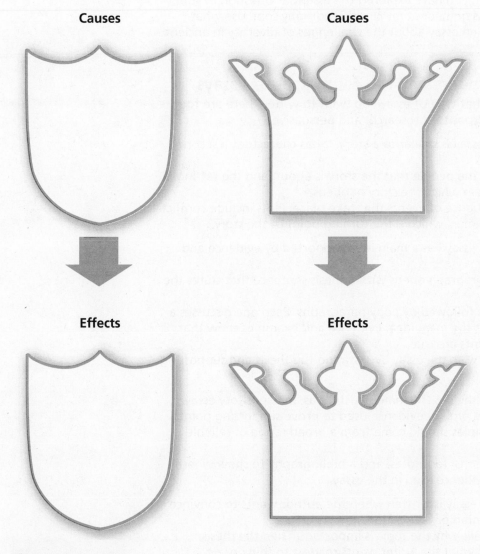

The Crusades

Causes

Effects

Decline of Feudalism

Causes

Effects

 **Essential Question**

How did diversity have both positive and negative effects on Spain?

_____

_____

_____

Essential Question Writer's Workshop

What are the challenges of diversity?

Prepare to Write
Throughout this chapter, you have explored the Essential Question in your text, journal, and On Assignment at myWorldGeography.com. Use what you've learned to write an essay about the challenges of diversity in ancient or medieval Europe.

Workshop Skill: Understand the Four Types of Essays
First you must decide what type of essay you want to write. There are four essay types: narrative, expository, research, and persuasive.

Narrative Essay This essay is similar to a story. It has characters, a setting, and a plot.
- The characters are the people that the story is about, and the setting is the time and place in which the story happens.
- The plot is the sequence of events that take place. Plots include conflict and lead up to a climax, which is the turning point of the story.

Expository Essay This essay has a main idea supported by evidence and examples.
- An introductory paragraph opens with a thesis sentence that states the main idea.
- The introduction is followed by body paragraphs. Each one discusses a point that supports the main idea. Evidence and examples show that the supporting points are true.
- The conclusion sums up the essay by restating the thesis and supporting points.

Research Essay This essay has the same structure as an expository essay. The difference lies in the type of evidence used to prove supporting points.
- Evidence and examples should come from a broad range of reliable sources.
- Writers use quotations, footnotes, and a bibliography to show where they located the evidence used in the essay.

Persuasive Essay This essay is written when the author wants to convince readers to adopt an opinion or take action.
- The introduction tells why the topic is important. Then the thesis statement explains what the writer wants readers to think or do.
- In the body paragraphs, the writer uses both arguments and evidence to prove the supporting points.
- The conclusion reviews the main points and urges the reader to adopt the opinion or take the action mentioned.

Identify Essay Types Use what you have learned to identify the different essay types. Read the four descriptions in the table on the next page. In the column on the right, write if the essay described is a narrative, expository, research, or persuasive one.

Essay Description	Type
1. The essay urges people of different cultures to stop fighting and learn from each other. It offers examples of people who have gained new insights from other cultures.	_____
2. The essay examines whether nations with diverse populations develop more new inventions than those nations who have people who conform. It contains graphs, charts, statistics, and quotations. Sources are listed in footnotes.	_____
3. The essay states that education helps people learn to understand other cultures. It explains three general ways that this can occur.	_____
4. The essay tells a story about a neighborhood in which ethnic groups fight because of conflicting customs. The story ends when two neighbors reach a compromise.	_____

Plan Your Essay

Use the following questions to help you make some decisions about your essay.

1. What do I want to say about the challenges of diversity in ancient or medieval Europe?

_____

_____

2. Do I want to tell a story, explain an idea, present evidence, or persuade others about something?

_____

_____

3. What type of essay will best help me accomplish my goal?

_____

_____

Organize Your Essay

Now that you have decided on an essay type, outline your essay. Remember to have an introductory paragraph, three body paragraphs, and a conclusion. Review how to structure each of those paragraphs. Then create your outline.

Draft Your Essay

Write your essay using the outline you created. When you're done, proofread your essay.

Name _____ Class _____ Date _____

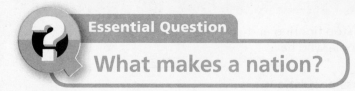

What makes a nation?

Preview Before you begin this chapter, think about the Essential Question. Understanding how the Essential Question connects to your life will help you understand the chapter you are about to read.

Connect to Your Life

(1) Think about foreign nations that you have visited, read about, or seen in TV shows and movies. What makes those nations different from the United States?

Things That Make Nations Different From Each Other			
Institutions	Geography	Culture	Other

Connect to the Chapter

(2) Suppose you are going to start a new nation. What are the essential things that your nation would need? Before you read the chapter, flip through every page and note the red headings, maps, and other pictures. Use your preview of the chapter to consider what you would need and record your ideas on the concept web.

(3) Now predict the ways that European countries have defined and expressed their nationhood. Record your ideas on the concept web using a different color pen or pencil.

(4) After reading the chapter, return to this page. Were your predictions accurate? Why or why not?

_____

_____

_____

Name _____ Class _____ Date _____

Connect to myStory: The Battle of the Spanish Armada

① Write a brief summary of the story about Elizabeth I and the Spanish Armada.

_____

_____

② Record the main events of the story on the cause-and-effect chart below.

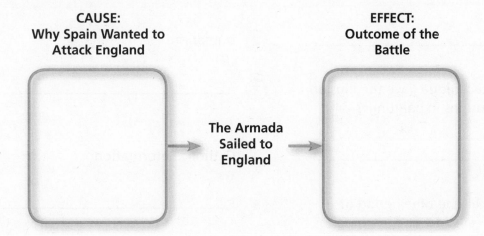

CAUSE:
Why Spain Wanted to
Attack England

The Armada
Sailed to
England

EFFECT:
Outcome of the
Battle

③ What do you think was the long-term impact of England's victory? Explain.

_____

_____

_____

Word Wise

Vocabulary Quiz Show Some quiz shows a question and expect the contestant to give the answer. In other shows the contestant is given an answer and must supply the question. If the blank is in the question column, write the question that would result in the answer in the answer column. If the answer is supplied, write the appropriate question.

QUESTION

ANSWER

1. What do you call the movement that led to the formation of Protestant churches?

1. _____

2. _____

2. humanism

3. What artistic technique gave the illusion of three dimensions in paintings?

3. _____

4. _____

4. Catholic Reformation

5. What do you call the time period of renewed interest in art and learning in Europe?

5. _____

Name _____ Class _____ Date _____

Take Notes

Map Skills Use the maps in *all* sections of this chapter to make a key and to label the Places to Know on the outline map below. Remember, in addition to this section, you will need to refer to Sections 2 through 5.

Places to Know!		
Countries		• **Cities**
England	Poland	• Wittenberg
Scotland	Romania	• Paris
Sweden	Belgium	• London
Spain		• Constantinople
Italy		• Berlin

KEY

0   400 mi

0   400 km

Lambert Conformal Conic Projection

Essential Question

How might a desire to build a stronger nation affect a ruler's decision to become a Protestant or a Catholic?

_____

_____

_____

Word Wise

Sentence Builder Complete the sentences using the information you learned in this section. Include terminal punctuation.

(1) **Absolutism** allowed European kings _____

_____

(2) The **caravel** helped the Portuguese _____

_____

(3) On the Spanish **plantations**, which were _____,

farmers _____

_____

(4) The **triangular trade** was _____

_____

(5) Advances in **cartography** led to _____

_____

(6) _____ searched for the **Northwest Passage**

because _____

_____

Name _____ Class _____ Date _____

Take Notes

Sequence Record events from the history of Europe on the timeline below.

1488

1492

1497

1513

1588

1740

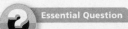

Essential Question

How might wars among European powers have helped build loyalty to the new nation-states?

_____

_____

_____

143

Word Wise

Words In Context For each question below, write an answer that shows your understanding of the boldfaced key term.

1 What major changes took place during the **Scientific Revolution**?

_____

_____

_____

2 During the **Enlightenment**, what methods did scholars use to study human nature?

_____

_____

_____

3 How did the **English Bill of Rights** affect the power of English monarchs?

_____

_____

_____

4 What event led to the start of the **French Revolution** and why?

_____

_____

_____

5 During the **Industrial Revolution**, how did the ways things were made change?

_____

_____

_____

Name _____ Class _____ Date _____

Take Notes

Cause and Effect Use the graphic organizer below to record the causes and effects of the Scientific Revolution, the French Revolution, and the Industrial Revolution.

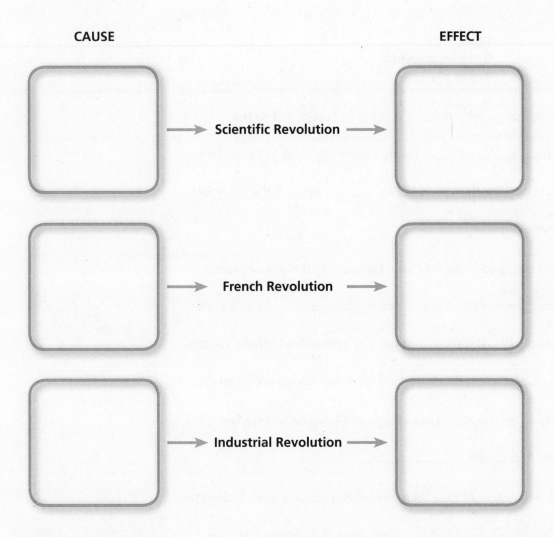

CAUSE

EFFECT

Scientific Revolution

French Revolution

Industrial Revolution

Essential Question

How did the Napoleonic Wars encourage nationalistic feelings in Europe?

_____

_____

_____

145

Word Wise

Word Bank Choose one word from the word bank to fill in each blank. When you have finished, you will have a short summary of important ideas from the section.

Word Bank

communism	fascism
Holocaust	Great Depression
World War I	World War II

Nationalistic rivalry and a military buildup in Europe led to the

outbreak of _____. Russia's suffering during the conflict

caused a revolution in which _____ became the basis for

the new government.

After being defeated in World War I, Germany had many economic

problems, which grew much worse during the _____. The

problems caused people to want a stronger government, and many citizens

thought that _____ would solve Germany's problems.

A political party called the Nazis took charge of Germany and started

another huge conflict called _____.

The Nazis, led by Adolf Hitler, were prejudiced against Jews. During the

war, the Nazis tried to eliminate all European Jews in a program of mass

murder called the _____. For the second time in 30 years,

the Allies defeated Germany in a global war.

Name _____ Class _____ Date _____

Take Notes

Compare and Contrast In this section, you read about two world wars.
Use the Venn diagram below to describe their similarities and differences.

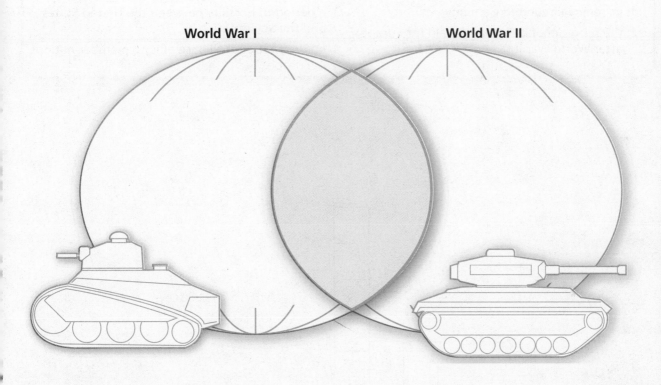

World War I   World War II

Essential Question

Why did so many nations gain independence after World War I?

_____

_____

_____

Word Wise

Crossword Puzzle The clues describe key terms from this section. Fill in the numbered *Across* boxes with the correct key terms. Then, do the same with the *Down* clues.

Across	Down
1. its removal reunited Germany	3. a period of hostility between the United States and the Soviet Union
2. the program of U.S. financial aid for Europe after World War II	4. an international alliance among member nations in Europe

Name _____ Class _____ Date _____

Take Notes

Main Ideas and Details Use what you have read in this section about Europe to complete the chart below. First, find the topic heading in the chapter. Write its main idea in your own words. Then give two details that support it.

Topic: Cold War and Division

Main idea:

Details:

1.

2.

Topic: The European Union

Main idea:

Details:

1.

2.

Topic: Democracy Spreads East

Main idea:

Details:

1.

2.

Topic: Europe Faces Challenges

Main idea:

Details:

1.

2.

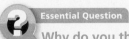

Essential Question

Why do you think East and West Germans still felt that they belonged to a single nation after more than 40 years apart?

_____

_____

_____

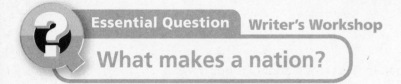

Essential Question Writer's Workshop

What makes a nation?

Prepare to Write

Throughout this chapter, you have explored the Essential Question in your text, journal, and On Assignment at myWorldGeography.com. Use these notes and what you have learned about Europe to write an essay detailing the elements that form a nation.

Workshop Skill: Use the Writing Process

Writing is a process with four different steps. However, it is not a linear process like baking a cake. You do not always have to do the steps in the same order or completely finish each step before starting the next. In writing, you can go back to earlier steps and do them over or add to what you did before. The four steps of the writing process are:

Prewrite Decide on a topic, brainstorm, gather information, take notes, and make an outline. While this is the first step, it is also one you may frequently revisit. When you are in the middle of drafting or revising, you may realize that you need to do more research.

Draft Working from your prewriting notes and outline, write the first draft of the essay. At this stage, you put your ideas into sentences and paragraphs. Remember that each paragraph needs a main idea expressed in a topic sentence. Other sentences support and explain that main idea. Use transitions to connect sentences within paragraphs and to show links between paragraphs.

Revise Reread your piece, looking for ways to improve the writing. Your goal is to make it as clear as possible. Make sure you have explained all your ideas completely. Ask yourself these questions: *Is the essay organized in the best way? Are the sentences too wordy?* Also, be sure you have used accurate nouns and active verbs. Be sure that your grammar and spelling are correct.

Present Prepare your final draft to share with others. Double space the manuscript. Include your name, the date, and the title of your piece. Again, proofread it carefully so that it is error free.

Prewrite

Let's practice the prewriting step. Review the notes you've taken and the assignments you've done related to the Essential Question, "What makes a nation?" Use the concept web below to brainstorm ideas.

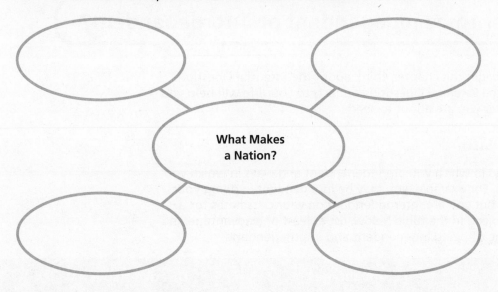

Create a Thesis Statement

Use the ideas from your concept web to write a thesis statement.

Thesis Statement _____

_____

Your thesis statement needs three supporting ideas:

1. _____

2. _____

3. _____

Draft Your Essay

Use the information you brainstormed above to write your essay on another piece of paper. You should have five paragraphs: an introduction, three body paragraphs, and a conclusion. Follow the steps in the writing process to revise, edit, and present your essay.

Essential Question

Is it better to be independent or interdependent?

Preview Before you begin this chapter, think about the Essential Question. Understanding how the Essential Question connects to your life will help you understand the chapter you are about to read.

Connect to Your Life

(1) Think about ways in which you are independent and ways in which you rely upon others. For example, you may be independent in doing your chores at home, but you are interdependent on your classmates for a school group project. In the table below, list at least one advantage and one disadvantage of being independent and interdependent.

	Advantages	Disadvantages
Independent		
Interdependent		

(2) Think of a situation in which you might act alone for part of the time and act with a group for part of the time. What are the advantages of combining independence and interdependence?

_____

_____

Connect to the Chapter

(3) Before you read the chapter, flip through every page. Note the boldfaced headings, maps, and other pictures. Try to predict areas in which European nations act independently and areas in which they act together. Record your predictions in the Venn diagram below.

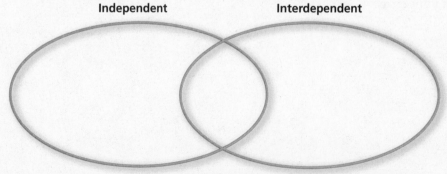

Independent   Interdependent

(4) After reading the chapter, circle your predictions that were accurate.

Name _____ Class _____ Date _____

Connect to myStory: Europe at Her Doorstep

(1) In the table below, list the different cultures that are part of Yasmin's background. Then list details about how each culture influences her daily life.

Culture	How It Influences Yasmin

(2) How was Yasmin's family affected by Sweden's decision to join the European Union?

_____

_____

(3) How do you think other Europeans have been affected by their country's membership in the European Union? Write your predictions below.

_____

_____

_____

Word Wise

Vocabulary Quiz Show Some quiz shows ask a question and expect the contestant to give the answer. In other shows, the contestant is given an answer and must supply the question. If the blank is in the question column, write the question that would result in the answer given. If the question is supplied, write the appropriate answer.

QUESTION

ANSWER

(1) What is the source of the streams that flow from the Alps?

(1) _____

(2) _____

(2) peninsula

(3) What type of flat or gently rolling landform stretches across much of Western Europe?

(3) _____

(4) _____

(4) tundra

(5) What is the name for the thick forest of coniferous trees in Northern Europe?

(5) _____

(6) _____

(6) pollution

(7) What is the word for Europe's rich soil made of sediments deposited by glaciers?

(7) _____

Name _____ Class _____ Date _____

Take Notes

Map Skills Use the maps in your book to make a key and to label the Places to Know the outline map below.

Places to Know!

Countries	City	Physical Features
France	London	Alps
Greece		Iberian Peninsula
Italy		North Sea
Iceland		Mediterranean Sea

KEY

0   400 mi

0   400 km

Lambert Conformal Conic Projection

Essential Question

Look at the languages map in this section. Do you think the number of languages spoken by EU members helps or harms Western Europe?

_____

_____

_____

Word Wise

Word Bank Choose one word from the word bank to fill in each blank. When you have finished, you will have a short summary of important ideas from the section.

Word Bank

constitutional monarchy   gross domestic product (GDP)
cultural borrowing   Parliament
cradle-to-grave system

The United Kingdom has a queen, but the _____

actually makes all the laws. Since the government is a

_____, the queen is just a ceremonial leader. The prime

minister is the real political leader of the nation.

Scandinavian countries have a _____ in which the

governments provide benefits for people of all ages. Scandinavia is so far

north that in the summer it has a period of almost 24-hour sunlight called

the white nights season.

The United Kingdom, Ireland, and the Scandinavian countries have all

experienced increasing numbers of immigrants, which leads to

_____. The countries in these regions are generally

economically prosperous. They have a high _____, which is

the total value of all goods and services produced and sold in a nation in one

year. A country with a high GDP often has a good standard of living for most

of its citizens.

Name _____ Class _____ Date _____

Take Notes

Compare and Contrast In this section, you read about the United Kingdom and the countries of Scandinavia. Use the Venn diagram below to describe how they are similar and how they differ.

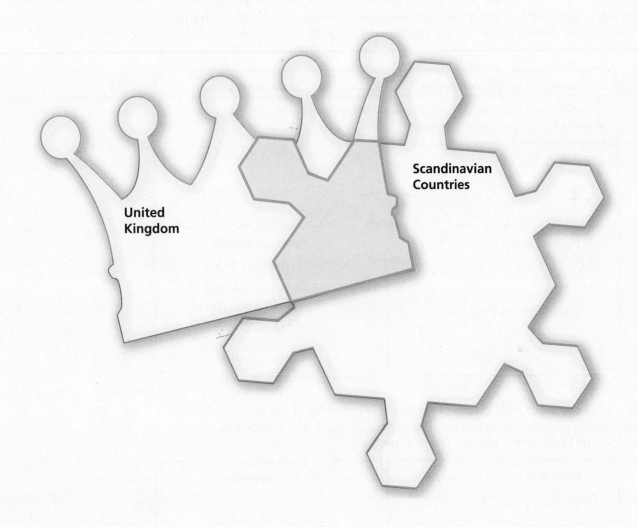

United Kingdom

Scandinavian Countries

Essential Question

What are the benefits of cultural borrowing? What might be some of the challenges?

_____

_____

_____

157

Word Wise

Word Map Follow the model below to make a word map. The key term *polders* is in the center oval. Write the definition in your own words at the upper left. In the upper right, list Characteristics, which means words or phrases that relate to the term. At the lower left list Noncharacteristics, which means words and phrases that would not be associated with it. In the lower right, draw a picture of the key term or use it in a sentence.

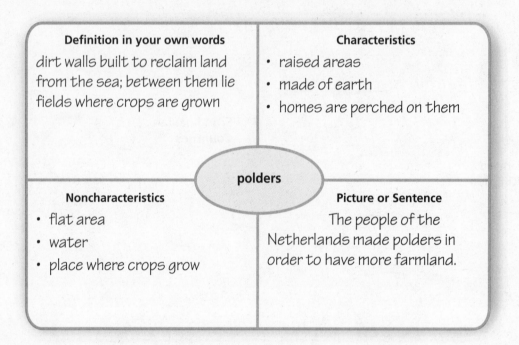

Definition in your own words	Characteristics
dirt walls built to reclaim land from the sea; between them lie fields where crops are grown	• raised areas • made of earth • homes are perched on them

polders

Noncharacteristics	Picture or Sentence
• flat area • water • place where crops grow	The people of the Netherlands made polders in order to have more farmland.

Now use the word map below to explore the meaning of the word *reunification*. You may use your student text, a dictionary, and/or a thesaurus to complete each of the four sections.

Definition in your own words	Characteristics

reunification

Noncharacteristics	Picture or Sentence

Make word maps of your own on a separate piece of paper for the following words: *privatization* and *gross national product (GNP)*.

Name _____ Class _____ Date _____

Take Notes

Main Ideas and Details In this section, you read about the countries of West Central Europe. Use the concept web below to record main ideas and details about the region's culture and international partnerships.

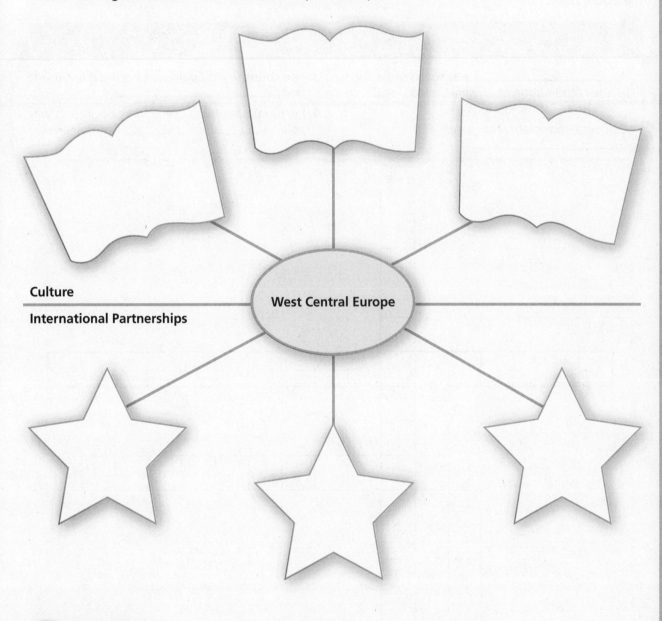

Culture

International Partnerships

West Central Europe

Essential Question

Why might EU membership appeal to smaller countries?

_____

_____

_____

Word Wise

Crossword Puzzle The clues describe key terms from this section. Fill in the numbered *Across* boxes with the correct key terms. Then, do the same with the *Down* clues.

Across	Down
1. _____ was responsible for the combination of Muslim, Jewish, and Christian influences in Spain.	3. The countries of Spain and Portugal are found on the _____.
2. Illegal immigrants fear arrest and _____.	4. Portugal has a strong economy because it was able to _____ its industries.

Name _____ Class _____ Date _____

Take Notes

Cause and Effect In this section, you read about Greece, Italy, Portugal, and Spain. Use the flowchart below to record the causes and effects of economic change and immigration in Southern Europe.

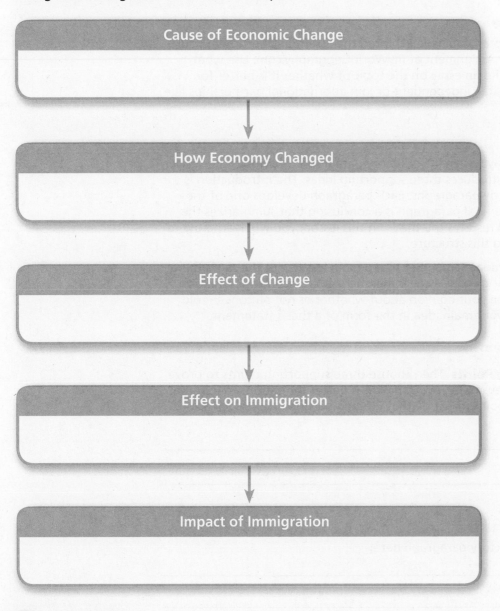

Cause of Economic Change

How Economy Changed

Effect of Change

Effect on Immigration

Impact of Immigration

? Essential Question

Has the European Union helped Southern Europe? Explain why or why not.

_____

_____

_____

Essential Question Writer's Workshop

Is it better to be independent or interdependent?

Prepare to Write

Throughout this chapter, you have explored the Essential Question in your text, journal, and On Assignment at myWorldGeography.com. Use what you've learned to write an essay on the topic of whether it is better for European nations to stay independent or join international partnerships like the European Union.

Workshop Skill: Outline An Essay

A five-paragraph essay has an introductory paragraph that hooks the reader, states a thesis, and introduces three supporting ideas. The introduction is followed by three body paragraphs. Each paragraph develops one of the supporting ideas. The final paragraph is a conclusion that summarizes the supporting ideas and restates the thesis. In this lesson, you will learn how to outline an essay using this structure.

Identify the Main Idea Remember that a main idea is not the same thing as the topic. The topic of your essay is membership in the European Union. Your main idea will be your *opinion* about whether or not nations should join the EU. Express your main idea in the form of a thesis statement.

Write a Thesis Statement _____

Choose Supporting Points Then choose three supporting points to prove your statement. For example, if you think it is better for nations to join the EU, one supporting point might be that EU membership encourages trade.

_____

_____

Outline the Introductory Paragraph

Outline your introductory paragraph here:

Hook _____

Thesis Statement _____

Sentence Summarizing the Supporting Ideas _____

Outline Body Paragraphs

Each paragraph needs a topic sentence that states the main idea. Include evidence to support the main idea. End the paragraph with a concluding sentence that tells how the information supports your thesis statement.

Body Paragraph 1
Topic sentence

_____

_____

Supporting detail

_____

_____

Supporting detail(s)

_____

_____

Concluding sentence

_____

_____

Follow this format to write two more body paragraphs.

Outline Your Conclusion

In the conclusion, you review your thesis, summarize your supporting points, explain how those points proved your statement, and end by telling the reader why this topic matters.

Paragraph 5: Conclusion

Restate the Thesis _____

Summary of Supporting Points _____

What the Supporting Points Prove _____

Why the Topic Matters _____

Draft Your Essay

Write your essay on your own paper. When you have finished, proofread it with a partner.

Name _____ Class _____ Date _____

How can you measure success?

Preview Before you begin this chapter, think about the Essential Question. Understanding how the Essential Question connects to your life will help you understand the chapter you are about to read.

Connect to Your Life

1. What does success mean to you? Think of some ways to measure success in the categories shown in the table below. List at least one way in each column. For example, under sports, you could list winning a major game in your favorite sport.

Measures of Personal Success			
Sports	Arts & Drama	Hobbies	Relationships

2. Think about what it takes to achieve success. Is it more difficult to reach some goals than others? Does this change the value of the success?

_____

_____

Connect to the Chapter

3. Before you read the chapter, flip through every page and note the red headings, maps, and pictures. What factors might limit success in Eastern Europe? What factors might encourage success? Use two different colored pens or pencils to list these factors on the table below.

Measures of National Success			
Economy	Politics	Social Services	Environment

4. Read the chapter. Review the predictions you made in the table above. Circle the ones that were correct.

Name _____ Class _____ Date _____

Connect to myStory: Serhiy's Leap

(1) Think about ways that your life is like Serhiy's life. What challenges does your family face daily? How does school play a role in your life? What are your hopes for the future?

_____

_____

(2) Use this Venn diagram to compare your life with Serhiy's life. Think about family challenges, school, and hopes for the future.

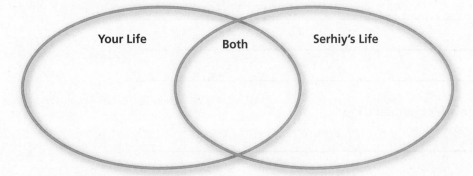

Your Life   Both   Serhiy's Life

(3) In the table below, list the challenges Serhiy faces as he tries to help his family meet its goals.

Daily Life	Making a Living	Getting an Education

(4) How do you think these challenges are affecting the people and nations of Eastern Europe?

_____

_____

_____

Word Wise

Words In Context For each question below, write an answer that shows your understanding of the boldfaced key term.

(1) Why have so many Eastern European Jews chosen to **emigrate**?

_____

_____

_____

(2) What happens during an **ice age**?

_____

_____

_____

(3) How can **acid rain** affect farmland?

_____

_____

_____

(4) What kind of land is best for **mechanized farming** and why?

_____

_____

_____

Name _____ Class _____ Date _____

Take Notes

Map Skills Use the maps in your book to make a key and to label the Places
to Know on the outline map below.

Places to Know!		
Physical Features	**Bodies of Water**	**Countries**
Balkan Mountains	• Black Sea	• Poland
North European Plain	• Baltic Sea	• Ukraine
Great Hungarian Plain	• Danube River	• Bosnia
		• Herzegovina

KEY

0 _____ 200 mi

0 _____ 200 km

Lambert Conformal Conic Projection

Essential Question

To join the European Union, countries must meet certain
environmental standards. Do you think protecting the environment
should be one measure of a country's success? Why or why not?

_____

_____

_____

Word Wise

Vocabulary Quiz Show Some quiz shows ask a question and expect the contestant to give the answer. In other shows, the contestant is given an answer and must supply the question. If the blank is in the question column, write the question that would result in the answer given. If the question is supplied, write the appropriate answer.

QUESTION

(1) What do you call a person who sets up and manages his or her own business?

(2) _____

(3) If one part of a country breaks away from that country and declares itself a new nation, what is that action called?

(4) _____

(5) What is the word for a specific style of food?

ANSWER

(1) _____

(2) ethnic cleansing

(3) _____

(4) capital

(5) _____

Name _____ Class _____ Date _____

Take Notes

Compare and Contrast In this section, you read how different countries and parts of Eastern Europe have succeeded, while others have faced challenges. In the table below, record the successes and the challenges in each section of Eastern Europe.

	Successes	Challenges
Poland and the Baltic Nations		
Central Europe		
The Balkan Nations		
Ukraine, Belarus, and Moldova		

Essential Question

Give an example of one Eastern European nation that has been successful in recent years. Why do you think this country has been successful?

_____

_____

_____

_____

Name _____ Class _____ Date _____

How can you measure success?

Prepare to Write

Throughout this chapter, you have explored the Essential Question in your text, journal, and On Assignment at myWorldGeography.com. Use what you've learned to write a compare and contrast essay about how any two countries in the region have changed since the fall of the Soviet Union. Consider how each of these factors has influenced each nation's progress: physical geography and natural resources; ethnic groups; conflict/war; economic goals; and government actions.

Workshop Skill: Write an Introduction and Thesis Statement

In this lesson, you will learn more about developing a thesis and introduction for your essay. A thesis is the main point you want to make in your essay. It is neither a topic nor a title. It is an idea that you will explain in the essay. Writers generally state their thesis in the introduction. Why? The first paragraph is like an outline to your essay. It tells readers your main point and briefly lists the arguments you will make to support it.

Determine the Essay Type Think about the characteristics of the type of essay you will write. Look for signal words in the essay question. For example, the words *compare and contrast* tell you that your essay must identify and explain ways in which two countries are similar and different. This means you must give facts about both countries and then explain how the information is related.

Write a Thesis Statement Consider the main point you want to make in your essay and phrase it as a thesis statement. Here's an example: *After achieving independence from the Soviet Union, the Czech Republic had more success than Slovakia*. This statement is specific to the question and mentions two nations: the Czech Republic and Slovakia. The rest of the essay will describe the success of the Czech Republic and the success of Slovakia, discussing reasons for the different outcomes the two nations have achieved. The thesis statement may appear at the start or at the end of your introduction.

Build the Introduction An introduction tells readers what your essay will be about and why they should care about the topic. Thus, you must give readers a little background. For example, you might explain that Czechoslovakia was controlled by the Soviet Union until 1990. In 1993 it split into the Czech Republic and Slovakia. Briefly state the main points the whole essay will make. You might choose to do this with one sentence describing the overall success of one nation and then another sentence explaining the success of the other nation. Finally, tell your readers why the topic is important.

Revise Your Thesis as You Write Sometimes as you explain your arguments, you may find that they don't exactly support the thesis. You may also change your topic a little bit. Keep checking and revising your thesis as you write. For example, in the sample thesis statement, you might replace *more success* with *success more quickly*. This adds a time element to the comparison.

As you revise your thesis, remember that it must:
- fit the essay assignment
- be clearly stated and easy to understand
- be supported by facts and logic

Here is a sample thesis and introduction:

Thesis *After becoming independent from the Soviet Union, the Czech Republic achieved success more quickly than Slovakia.*

Background *Until 1990, these two nations had been the Soviet-controlled nation called Czechoslovakia. They split into two separate nations in 1993.*

Main Point 1 *Historical circumstances favored the Czech Republic. The nation's leaders also increased their advantage with aggressive modernization policies.*

Main Point 2 *The Czech Republic had a diverse economy with many different industries which allowed for rapid modernization.*

Main Point 3 *Slovakia, however, had just one main industry. When that industry slowed, it hindered the modernization of the rest of the economy.*

Why it Matters *The history of these two countries since 1993 provides lessons about why countries struggle or succeed.*

Create Your Thesis and Introduction
Now write your own thesis and introduction.

Sample thesis _____

_____

Background _____

_____

Main Point 1 _____

_____

Main Point 2 _____

_____

Why it Matters _____

_____

Draft Your Essay
Use the thesis and introduction in your essay, which will be written on another paper. Complete your essay, and proofread it with a partner.

Name _____ Class _____ Date _____

What should governments do?

Preview Before you begin this chapter, think about the Essential Question. Understanding how the Essential Question connects to your life will help you understand the chapter you are about to read.

Connect to Your Life

(1) Think of different ways in which the United States government affects your life. List at least one way in each column. For example, under laws you could list laws that prohibit stealing.

How the United States Government Affects My Life				
Laws	• Taxes	• Military	• Environment	• Transportation

(2) Look at the table. Do you think the government should be doing everything you listed? Is there something that you think the government should do that it isn't doing? Write your ideas here.

_____

Connect to the Chapter

(3) Nations sometimes go through bad times such as wars or economic slowdowns. Do you think a government should take different actions during bad times than it does during good times? Record your ideas on the Venn diagram below.

What should governments do?

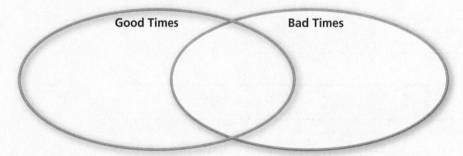

Good Times   Bad Times

(4) Before you read the chapter, flip through every page and note the red headings, maps, and other pictures. Now record your predictions of what actions the Russian government will take during bad times on the Venn diagram above using a different colored ink or pencil.

(5) At the end of the chapter, come back to this page. Circle any accurate predictions you made.

Name _____ Class _____ Date _____

Connect to myStory: Boris's Big Spin

(1) Fill in the table below to compare your life to Boris's life in each of the five areas listed.

How Our Lives Compare		
	My Life	Boris's Life
Family		
Travel		
Social Pressure		
Sports/Hobbies		
Military Conflict		

(2) Look at what you wrote in the table above. Tell one way in which your life is easier than Boris's. Explain.

_____

_____

_____

(3) Look at the table again. Tell one way in which your life is harder than Boris's. Explain.

_____

_____

_____

(4) What does Boris's story tell you about life in Russia today?

_____

_____

_____

173

Word Wise

Word Bank Choose one word from the word bank to fill in each blank. When you have finished, you will have a short summary of important ideas from the section.

Word Bank

Ural Mountains	Siberia
Lake Baikal	steppes
permafrost	Kamchatka Peninsula

Russia is the largest nation on Earth; it stretches almost halfway around the globe! In fact, it lies on two continents: Europe and Asia. Although they are not very tall, the _____ separate Russia into European Russia and Asiatic Russia. Asiatic Russia is also called _____.

Russia has large grasslands, or _____, which is where its farmland is found. One of the challenges for Russia is that that much of its soil is _____, or permanently frozen soil beneath the tundra and taiga biomes. This makes constructing roads, railroads, and buildings difficult or even impossible.

Russia has some of the most interesting geographical features in the world. There are 160 volcanoes on Russia's _____, and 29 of them are active! The nation's huge _____ holds about 20 percent of Earth's freshwater. It contains more water than our five Great Lakes combined.

Name _____ Class _____ Date _____

Take Notes

Map Skills Use the maps in your book to make a key and to label the Places to Know on the outline map below.

Places to Know!	
Physical Features	**Region**
Kamchatka Peninsula	Siberia
Ural Mountains	
Lake Baikal	
Kuril Islands	

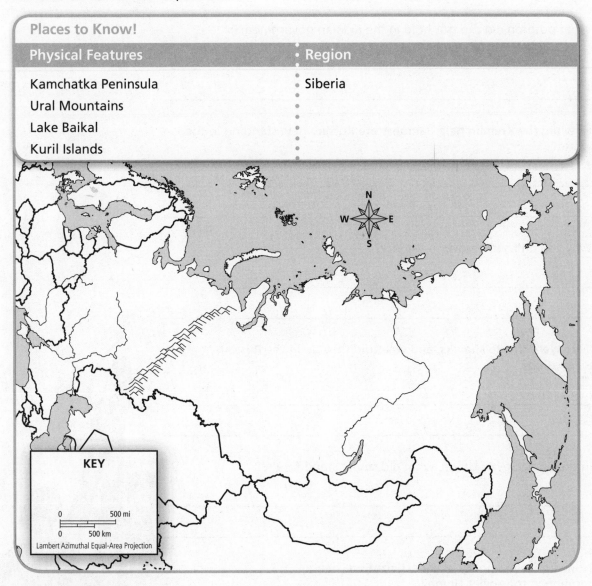

KEY

0 — 500 mi
0 — 500 km
Lambert Azimuthal Equal-Area Projection

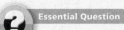 **Essential Question**

Look at the railroad mileage chart in this section. The Russian government helped pay the cost of building the Trans-Siberian Railroad. Why might governments invest in transportation systems?

_____

_____

_____

Word Wise

Words in Context For each question below, write an answer that shows your understanding of the boldfaced key term.

(1) What position did the **tsar** hold in the Russian government?

_____

_____

(2) How did the **Kremlin** help demonstrate Russia's new standing in the world?

_____

_____

(3) Why couldn't **serfs** move to the city?

_____

_____

(4) Who were the **Bolsheviks**, and what did they do in the Russian Revolution?

_____

_____

(5) In the name Soviet Union, what did **soviet** stand for?

_____

_____

(6) How did Stalin's policy of **collectivization** change farming in the Soviet Union?

_____

_____

Name _____ Class _____ Date _____

Take Notes

Cause and Effect Use the cause-and-effect boxes below to record information about the Russian Revolution and the fall of the Soviet Union.

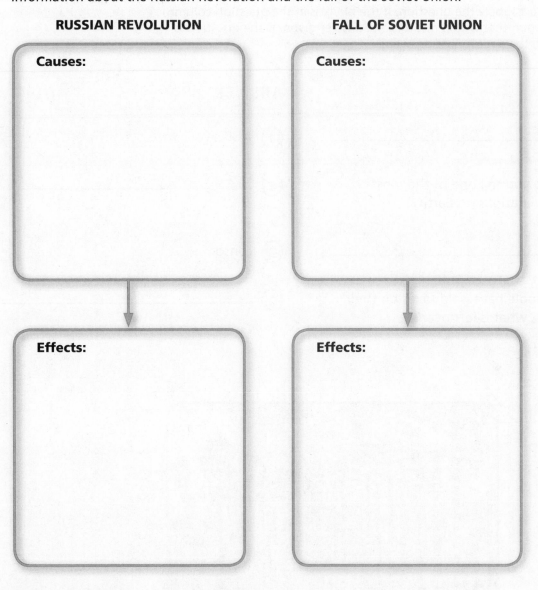

RUSSIAN REVOLUTION

FALL OF SOVIET UNION

Causes:

Causes:

Effects:

Effects:

Essential Question

Think about the famines that have occurred throughout Russian history. What actions might a government take during disasters such as famines?

_____

_____

_____

Word Wise

Vocabulary Quiz Show Some quiz shows ask a question and expect the contestant to give the answer. In other shows, the contestant is given an answer and must supply the question. If the blank is in the question column, write the question that would result in the answer given. If the question is supplied, write the appropriate answer.

QUESTION

ANSWER

(1) _____

(1) KGB

(2) What do you call one of the most powerful nations on Earth?

(2) _____

(3) _____

(3) censor

(4) After people have paid taxes on their earnings, what is left over?

(4) _____

Name _____ Class _____ Date _____

Take Notes

Main Ideas and Details In this section, you read about the many challenges faced by Russia today. Use the concept web below to record main ideas and details about those events.

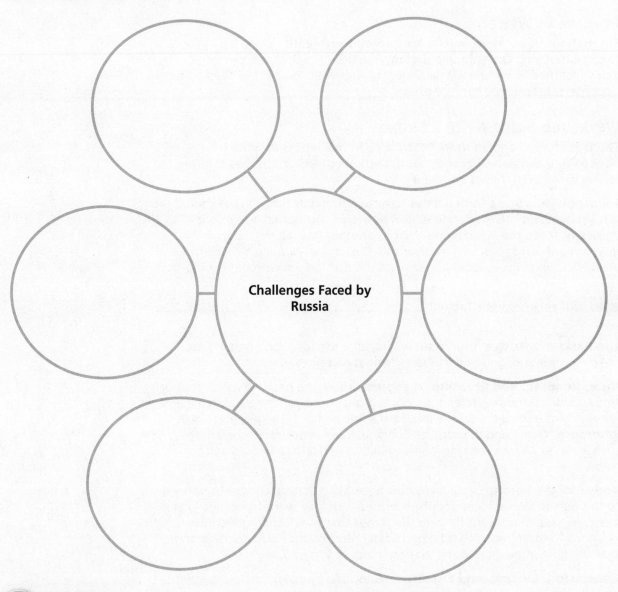

Challenges Faced by
Russia

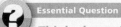 **Essential Question**

Think about the life expectancy and infant mortality graphs in this section. What do you think the government can do about the health problems in Russia?

_____

_____

_____

What should governments do?

Prepare to Write

Throughout this chapter, you have explored the Essential Question in your text, journal, and On Assignment at myWorldGeography.com. Use what you've learned to write a formal letter stating what you believe the Russian government should do for its citizens.

Workshop Skill: Write a Letter

There are formal and informal letters. Use formal letters to write to newspapers, businesses, governments, and other institutions. Use informal letters to write to friends and family.

Today you will write a formal letter to answer the question, "What should governments do?" First, decide who will receive your letter. You might write a letter to the Russian president to another Russian politician or government official, or to the editor of a Russian newspaper. Your purpose will be to explain your ideas about what the Russian government should do.

Who will receive your letter? _____

The Parts of a Letter Your letter will include the following parts: date, heading, greeting, body, conclusion, closing, and signature.

Date, Heading, and Greeting In a formal letter, the heading includes your return address and the date in the upper right corner, and the full name and address of the recipient on the left. Skip a line and put the greeting. Most letters use "Dear" and the recipient's name. In a formal letter, use a title such as *Dr.* or *Mrs.* or *Senator* followed by the person's last name and a colon.

Body Use the body to explain your purpose. Why did you choose to write to this person? What ideas about government do you want to express? For example, you might want to state the things that the Russian government has done in recent years that helped its people. You may also discuss things that the government has done that has hindered its people.

Conclusion, Closing, and Signature Conclude by briefly restating your main point. If you want the recipient to take action, such as working to pass a law or printing your letter in the newspaper, state that. Below the conclusion, skip a line, write a closing such as "Sincerely yours," or "Yours truly," followed by a comma. Sign your full name below it.

Draft Your Letter

Use the format below to write the first draft of your letter.

(your address and date; do not put your name)
_____
_____
_____

_____ **(name and address of recipient)**
_____
_____
_____

Dear _____

Body _____
_____
_____
_____
_____

Conclusion _____
_____
_____
_____

Closing _____

Your signature _____

Finalize Your Letter

Remember to follow the steps of the writing process to revise and edit your letter. Then neatly copy it onto a clean sheet of paper.

Name _____ Class _____ Date _____

Who should benefit from a country's resources?

Preview Before you begin this chapter, think about the Essential Question. Understanding how the Essential Question connects to your life will help you understand the chapter you are about to read.

Connect to Your Life

1. How do you and your friends share? Think about sharing a bag of candy, taking turns playing a game, or sharing an object. What are the positives and negatives of different ways of sharing?

Different Ways to Share

Sharing Strategy	Equal portion for all	Biggest appetite gets more	More for those who pay more	Other
Pros				
Cons				

Connect to the Chapter

2. Before you read the chapter, flip through every page. Note the headings, maps, and pictures. Then, predict how each of these sharing strategies might work when different countries try them.

_____

_____

3. Read the chapter. Think of how countries in West and Central Africa have shared resources in the ways shown in the chart below. Write yes or no in the first row. For those columns in which the answer is yes, write the name of the nation or group that used it in the second row.

Ways to Divide Resources in the Real World

Sharing Strategy	Shares are based on need.	Wealthy and powerful people take more than others.	Everybody fights.
Used in West and Central Africa?			
Name (if yes)			

Name _____ Class _____ Date _____

Connect to myStory:
A String of Dreams

① Think about a major store or a mall in your community. Where do the goods they sell come from? How do they get there?

_____

_____

_____

② List five facts about Ghana that you learned from reading Evelyn's story.

Fact 1	Fact 2	Fact 3	Fact 4	Fact 5

③ Based on Evelyn's story, predict if trade and commerce were important in the history of West and Central Africa. Do you think that trade and commerce have a major role in life there today? Why or why not?

_____

_____

_____

_____

Word Wise

Sentence Builder Complete the sentences using the information you learned in this section. Include terminal punctuation.

① **Desertification** is one of the biggest worries in the **Sahel** because

_____

_____

② On the African **savanna** the land is _____ and the

vegetation is _____

_____

③ **Malaria** is a(n) _____ spread by _____

and is common in _____

_____

④ **Deforestation** means _____ and is threatening to

cause **desertification** in the nations of _____

_____

⑤ A major problem threatening Africa is that **arable land** can become

_____

Name _____ Class _____ Date _____

Take Notes

Map Skills Use the maps in your book to make a key and to label the Places to Know on the outline map below.

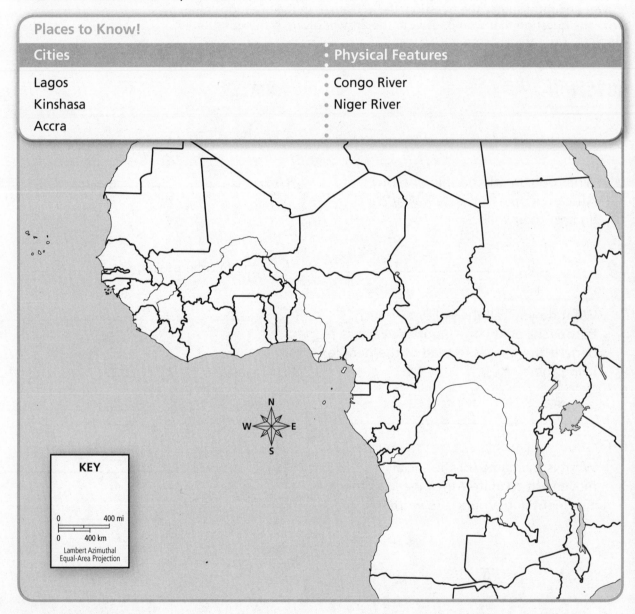

Places to Know!

Cities	Physical Features
Lagos	Congo River
Kinshasa	Niger River
Accra	

KEY

0   400 mi

0   400 km

Lambert Azimuthal
Equal-Area Projection

Essential Question

How might not having abundant farmland or natural resources affect a county?

_____

_____

_____

185

Word Wise

Vocabulary Quiz Show Some quiz shows ask a question and expect the contestant to give the answer. In other shows, the contestant is given an answer and must supply the question. If the blank is in the question column, write the question that would result in the answer given. If the question is supplied, write the appropriate answer.

QUESTION	ANSWER
(1) _____	(1) the salt trade
(2) What do you call the shipping of African people to the New World against their will?	(2) _____
(3) _____	(3) the middle passage
(4) What do you call the policy by which Europeans built large empires overseas to benefit themselves instead of the people living there?	(4) _____
(5) _____	(5) colonialism
(6) What is the name for the social movement to unite Africans across the continent and around the world?	(6) _____

Name _____ Class _____ Date _____

Take Notes

Sequence Label each range of dates on the timeline with the event that happened or a state that existed in West and Central Africa during that period. Fill in two facts about each event or state.

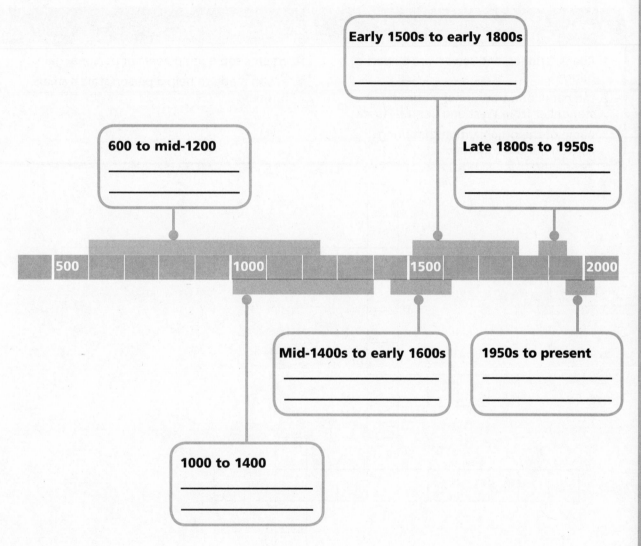

Early 1500s to early 1800s
_____
_____

600 to mid-1200
_____
_____

Late 1800s to 1950s
_____
_____

500   1000   1500   2000

Mid-1400s to early 1600s
_____
_____

1950s to present
_____
_____

1000 to 1400
_____
_____

Essential Question

What role did natural resources play in the history of West and Central Africa?

_____
_____
_____

Word Wise

Crossword Puzzle The clues describe key terms from this section. Fill in the numbered *Across* boxes with the correct key terms. Then, do the same with the *Down* clues.

Across

1. Roads, bridges, and sewers are all part of a nation's _____.
2. the name of a traditional musician-storyteller from West and Central Africa
3. name of the organization that brings African nations together

Down

4. when people use power for personal gain
5. a loan made to help a person start a small business

Name _____ Class _____ Date _____

Take Notes

Main Ideas and Details Use this table to help understand the main ideas of this section. Each box lists the name of a heading in this section. For each, write the main idea for that part and at least two supporting details about that main idea.

Economic Challenges	Political Challenges	Cultures of the Region	Hope for the Future

Essential Question

How does unequal access to oil wealth affect the lives of Nigeria's people?

_____

_____

_____

Essential Question Writer's Workshop

Who should benefit from a country's resources?

Prepare to Write

Throughout this chapter, you have explored the Essential Question in your text, journal, and On Assignment at myWorldGeography.com. Use what you've learned to write an essay on the topic of how people should handle resources in West and Central Africa. Consider the following: the resources that exist in the region, who benefits from them now, who benefited from them in the past, and the need for change in the region.

Workshop Skill: Write Body Paragraphs

Review how to outline your essay and write an introduction. Phrase the main point you want to make in your essay as a thesis statement. For example, *Nigeria does not use its resources wisely*. In your introduction, support your thesis with three facts.

In this lesson, you will learn how to write body paragraphs. Each body paragraph should develop one of the ideas you listed in the introduction that supports your thesis statement. Each body paragraph takes the idea further by giving details or evidence.

Write a Topic Sentence Start with a topic sentence. A topic sentence must clearly state the main idea of the body paragraph, connect that idea to the essay's thesis, and provide a transition from the previous paragraph. The sample body paragraph below was designed to follow the introduction paragraph.

Support the Topic Sentence With Discussion and Facts Explain your point and support it with discussion and details. Discussion sentences connect and explain your main point and supporting details. Supporting details provide the meat—the actual facts that show that what you say is true.

End With a Concluding Sentence Finish your paragraph with a sentence that reflects your topic sentence and draws together the details.

Here is a sample body paragraph:

Sample topic sentence *Nigeria does not use its resources wisely because it allows the oil industry to damage the environment.*

Supporting discussion *Although the oil industry is the country's biggest business, allowing it to harm the environment has serious consequences.*

Supporting detail *Air pollution from oil and natural gas makes the skies sooty and the air hard to breathe.*

Supporting detail *Due to pollution from oil fields, Nigerians can no longer fish in the Niger Delta.*

Supporting discussion *The loss of fish as a food source and the polluted air hurts the people living in the Niger Delta.*

Concluding sentence *To avoid these problems, Nigerians should prevent environmental damage from the oil industry.*

190

Write a Body Paragraph

Now write your own body paragraph for your essay.

Topic sentence

_____

_____

Supporting discussion

_____

_____

Supporting detail

_____

_____

Supporting detail

_____

_____

Supporting discussion

_____

_____

Concluding sentence

_____

_____

Draft Your Essay

Use the body paragraph above in your complete five-paragraph essay
(written on another sheet of paper). Check each of your body paragraphs
for a topic sentence, supporting details, and a concluding sentence.

Essential Question

Is conflict unavoidable?

Preview Before you begin this chapter, think about the Essential Question. Understanding how the Essential Question connects to your life will help you understand the chapter you are about to read.

Connect to Your Life

(1) What has caused conflicts in your family, school, community, or state? Name two recent conflicts.

_____

_____

(2) Listed in the table below are three reasons for conflicts. Rate how apt each one is to cause conflict, with 1 being likely and 5 being unlikely. To help decide, you may want to consider the conflicts you named above.

Reason for Conflict	How likely is it to cause conflict?				
Misunderstandings	1	2	3	4	5
Power struggles	1	2	3	4	5
Differences	1	2	3	4	5
Other: _____	1	2	3	4	5

Connect to the Chapter

(3) Now think about sources of conflict in a country. For example, differences in religious beliefs can lead to tension. Preview the chapter by skimming the chapter's headings, photographs, and graphics. In the web below, predict sources of conflict in Southern and Eastern Africa.

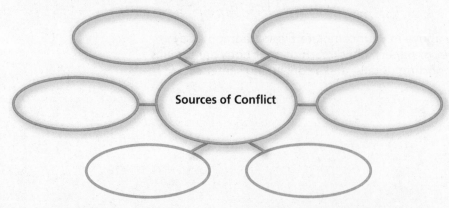

Sources of Conflict

(4) After reading the chapter, return to this page and use a highlighter to mark your accurate predictions.

Name _____ Class _____ Date _____

Connect to myStory:
A Hopeful Song

1 Think about ways in which your life is similar to and different from Khulekani's life. What challenges does your family face on a daily basis? How does school play a role in your life? What are your hopes for the future?

_____

_____

_____

2 Use this Venn diagram to compare your life with Khulekani's life. Think about family challenges, your school, and your hopes for the future.

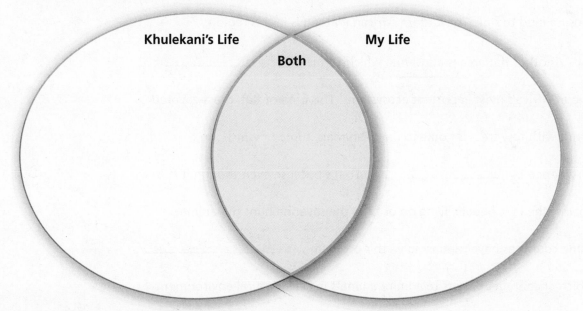

Khulekani's Life   Both   My Life

3 On the table below, list the challenges Khulekani faces as he tries to help his family meets its goals.

Daily Life	Earning a Living	Getting an Education

4 How do you think these challenges affect the people and nations of Southern and Eastern Africa? Write at least two ideas below.

_____

_____

Word Wise

Word Bank Choose one word from the word bank to fill in each blank. When you have finished, you will have a short summary of important ideas from the section.

Word Bank

Serengeti Plain   ecotourism
poaching   Great Rift Valley

Southern and Eastern Africa has physical features that support several

different ecosystems. One unusual physical feature is the

_____, which formed when two of Earth's plates separated,

causing land to sink. The Eastern African Plateau is in this region.

Another flat area is a savanna which forms the _____,

one of Africa's most important ecosystems. This area of flat, grass-covered

plains with few trees is home to many animals, some of which are

threatened by _____. That's because even though it is

against the law, people living on or near the savanna hunt the animals.

Some countries have tried to solve this problem with _____,

which encourages visitors to admire animals in their natural environment

without damaging the ecosystem.

Name _____ Class _____ Date _____

Take Notes

Map Skills Use the maps in your book to make a key and to label the Places to Know on the outline map below.

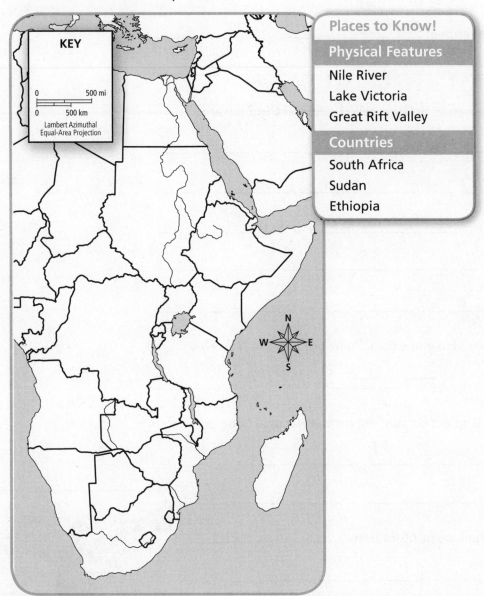

Places to Know!

Physical Features

Nile River

Lake Victoria

Great Rift Valley

Countries

South Africa

Sudan

Ethiopia

Essential Question

How do you think the lack of resources in some countries might cause conflict? How might the abundance of resources in other countries cause conflict?

_____

_____

_____

Word Wise

Sentence Builder Complete the sentences using the information you learned in this section. Include terminal punctuation.

① **Apartheid** was the result of _____

_____

② European colonists had an attitude called **ethnocentrism** toward

_____ because _____

_____

③ The **Boers** came from _____ and settled _____

_____

_____

④ Many Kenyans wanted to end colonial rule, but only the **Mau Mau**

_____

⑤ South Africa's government banned the **African National Congress**

because _____

_____

⑥ **Fossils** of ancient humans in Africa show _____

_____

THE RHODES COLOSSUS

Name _____ Class _____ Date _____

Take Notes

Sequence Use what you have read about the history of Southern and Eastern Africa to complete the timeline below. For each date given, write the event.

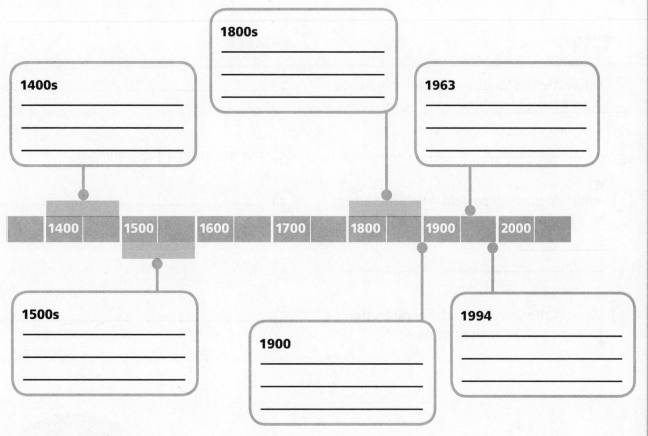

1800s
_____
_____
_____

1400s
_____
_____
_____

1963
_____
_____
_____

1500s
_____
_____
_____

1900
_____
_____
_____

1994
_____
_____
_____

1400   1500   1600   1700   1800   1900   2000

Essential Question

Apartheid in South Africa ended without civil war or large-scale ethnic conflict. What do you think made this possible?

_____

_____

_____

Word Wise

Vocabulary Quiz Show Some quiz shows ask a question and expect the contestant to give the answer. In other shows, the contestant is given an answer and must supply the question. If the blank is in the question column, write the question that would result in the answer given. If the question is supplied, write the appropriate answer.

QUESTION

1. What African language is basically Bantu with Arabic elements?

2. _____

3. What do you call people who are native to a region?

4. _____

5. What is the word for a deliberate attempt to wipe out an entire people?

ANSWER

1. _____

2. nongovernmental organization

3. _____

4. AIDS

5. _____

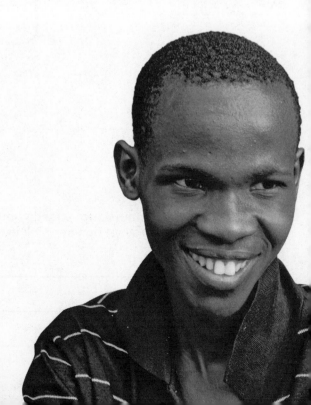

Name _____ Class _____ Date _____

Take Notes

Compare and Contrast Use what you read about life in Southern and
Eastern Africa today to complete the table below. For each factor listed, give
a contrasting example from the section. If the contrast between the two has
led to a conflict, circle yes in the last column. Otherwise, circle no. The first
row is completed for you.

Factor	Contrasting Examples		Has it Caused Conflict?
language	Swahili as a common language	English in former British colonies	Yes (No)
ethnicity		Africans in southern Sudan	Yes No
political system	single-party rule in Zimbabwe		Yes No

Look at the row(s) in which you circled yes. Write an explanation of why
these contrasts caused conflict.

_____

_____

_____

_____

Essential Question

In the countries of Sudan, Rwanda, Kenya, and South Africa, what
has caused ethnic violence?

_____

_____

_____

_____

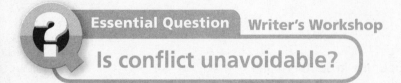

Essential Question   Writer's Workshop

Is conflict unavoidable?

Prepare to Write

Throughout this chapter, you have explored the Essential Question in your text, journal, and On Assignment at myWorldGeography.com. Use what you learned to write an essay about why the nations in Southern and Eastern Africa should teach their citizens to avoid conflict. Consider the following factors: ethnic, religious, and political differences that exist in the region, the economic challenges these countries face, the ways conflict has shaped African history, and the benefits of avoiding future conflicts.

Workshop Skill: Write a Conclusion

Review how to outline your essay, write an introduction, and develop body paragraphs. Consider the main point you want to make in your essay and phrase it as a thesis statement—for example: *Teaching people to avoid conflict will improve the future for Southern and Eastern Africa.* In your introduction, list three ideas that support this thesis. In your body paragraphs, develop one idea in each paragraph, using details and evidence to support it. For example, you might write *Conflict has interfered with Southern and Eastern Africa's ability to meet its economic challenges.* Follow this by giving specific examples of why the statement is true.

In this lesson, you will learn how to summarize your arguments in a conclusion. The conclusion of an essay has three goals: It must restate your thesis and tell readers why it matters to them. It must briefly acknowledge challenges to your argument and remind readers why your argument makes sense. Finally, it must tell readers what you want them to think or do.

Connect With a Restatement Start with a sentence that recalls your topic and thesis. Emphasize the importance of your argument by telling readers how the issue affects people outside the region. Remember to shape that sentence in a way that moves smoothly from the final body paragraph.

Answer Challenges With a Rebuttal Next, imagine you are debating your issue face to face. What arguments would someone give against your thesis? In one or two sentences, identify one of these arguments and explain why it is incorrect or not convincing. For example, you might note that it will cost money to teach new attitudes but that the poverty caused by conflict will actually cost more.

Call to Action Finish your conclusion with a specific request for action by answering the question: What can readers do to help solve the problem? Discuss ways that people can change their thinking. You may also describe some actions people can take.

Sample Conclusion

This conclusion demonstrates all three parts:

Restatement *For all these reasons, people around the world should support the goal of teaching Africans to avoid conflict. When African countries prosper, they will demand less international aid and contribute more to the global economy.*

Rebuttal *Of course teaching conflict avoidance will cost the rest of us money, but cleaning up the problems caused by African conflict will cost us much more in the long run.*

Call to Action *The nations of the world must think in terms of investing in a shared future and building a roof to shelter all of us. Write your Congressional representative today to promote funding for conflict-resolution programs in Africa.*

Draft Your Conclusion

Now write each part of the conclusion for your essay:

Restatement _____

_____

_____

_____

Rebuttal _____

_____

_____

_____

Call to Action _____

_____

_____

_____

Draft Your Essay

Make sure your conclusion restates your thesis, includes a response to anticipated challenges, and has a clearly stated call to action. Use your conclusion at the end of your five-paragraph essay. Write the essay on another piece of paper.

? Essential Question

How much does geography shape a country?

Preview Before you begin this chapter, think about the Essential Question. Understanding how the Essential Question connects to your life will help you understand the chapter you are about to read.

Connect to Your Life

(1) Think about how the geographic elements in the table below have affected your life. Complete the table below with your ideas.

Personal Influence of Geographic Elements				
Parks, Lakes, Rivers •	Local Weather •	Local Crops •	Size of School •	Recreational Activities

(2) In what ways can these elements affect each other? For example, in what way can cold weather affect the type of recreational activities in a region?

_____

_____

Connect to the Chapter

(3) Before you read the chapter, flip through every page and note the red headings, maps, and other pictures. Predict ways in which geography has influenced families and communities in North Africa. List your ideas in the table below.

Influences of Geographic Elements on a Country				
Physical Features	• Climate	• Natural Resources	• Population	• Culture

(4) After reading the chapter, return to this page. Were your predictions accurate? Why or why not?

_____

_____

Name _____ Class _____ Date _____

Connect to myStory: Shaimaa's Neighborhood

1. What challenges face your family every day? How does school play a role in your life? What are your hopes for the future?

   _____

   _____

2. Use this Venn diagram to compare your life with Shaimaa's life. Think about family challenges, school, and hopes for the future.

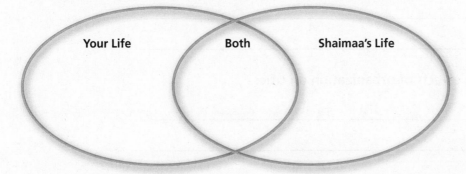

Your Life   Both   Shaimaa's Life

3. In this graphic organizer, list the challenges Shaimaa faces as she tries to help her family to meet its goals.

   Daily Life

   Making a Living

   Getting an Education

4. How do you think these challenges are affecting people in North Africa? Write your predictions.

   _____

   _____

Word Wise

Words In Context For each question below, write an answer that shows your understanding of the boldfaced key term.

(1) Why do people of the Sahara live near **oases**?

_____

_____

(2) How does a river change at its **delta**? How does a river's **delta** change the surrounding land?

_____

_____

(3) What are some effects of **urbanization** on cities?

_____

_____

(4) Why do **nomads** in the Sahara Desert live by herding animals instead of by farming?

_____

_____

Name _____ Class _____ Date _____

Take Notes

Map Skills Use the maps in your book to make a key and to label the Places to Know on the outline map below.

Places to Know!

Physical Features	Countries
Sahara Desert	Egypt
Atlas Mountains	Morocco
Nile River	Algeria
Suez Canal	

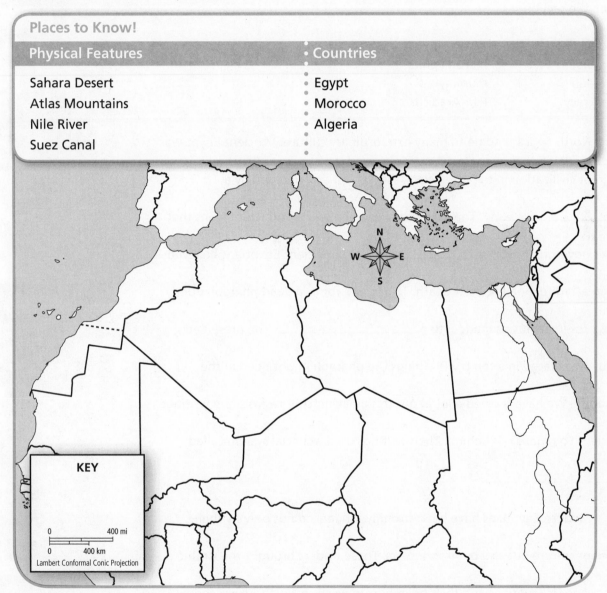

KEY

0 — 400 mi
0 — 400 km
Lambert Conformal Conic Projection

Essential Question

How does water shape human settlement patterns in North Africa?

_____

_____

_____

Word Wise

Word Bank Choose one word from the word bank to fill in each blank. When you have finished, you will have a short summary of important ideas from the section.

Word Bank

Berbers	hieroglyphics
pharaoh	mummy
theocracy	Pan-Arabism

North Africa is home to many extraordinary cultures. Ancient Egypt was a great civilization in the Nile River Valley. Egyptians were led by a _____. The citizens believed he was a god. This means that their government was a _____. Ancient Egyptians believed in an afterlife, or a life after death. To prepare for it, a dead pharaoh's body was preserved. It was made into a _____. The preserved body was placed in a tomb with things the pharaoh might need in the afterlife. We have learned a lot about this amazing culture from the writings ancient Egyptians left behind. Their writings used a special system called _____.

Modern Egyptians have been strongly influenced not only by their ancient culture but also by Arab traders. These traders brought the Arabic language to Egyptians and their neighbors in western North Africa, the _____. Today some people in the region support _____, or the idea that this common language should unite nations.

Name _____ Class _____ Date _____

Take Notes

Cause and Effect Use what you have read about the history of North Africa to complete the table below. Under each column, list effects of each culture on the history of North Africa.

Impact of Cultures on North Africa		
Ancient Egypt	Arab North Africa	European Rule

Essential Question

How did physical geography shape the development of ancient Egypt?

_____

_____

_____

Word Wise

Sentence Builder Complete the sentences using the information you learned in this section. Include terminal punctuation.

1. A nation's **gross domestic product** tells _____

_____

2. The **Copts**, who belong to a minority group in Egypt, are the largest

_____ in the Middle East, yet they are _____

_____

3. The **human development index** includes quality of life factors such as

_____

4. The **gross domestic product per capita** is a measure of _____

_____

5. Egyptians who belong to the **Muslim Brotherhood** _____

_____

6. Those who believe in **secularism** _____

_____

Name _____ Class _____ Date _____

Take Notes

Main Idea and Details Use what you read about the current governments and political issues in North Africa to complete this concept web. In each labeled oval, list details about that country's government and the political issues the country faces.

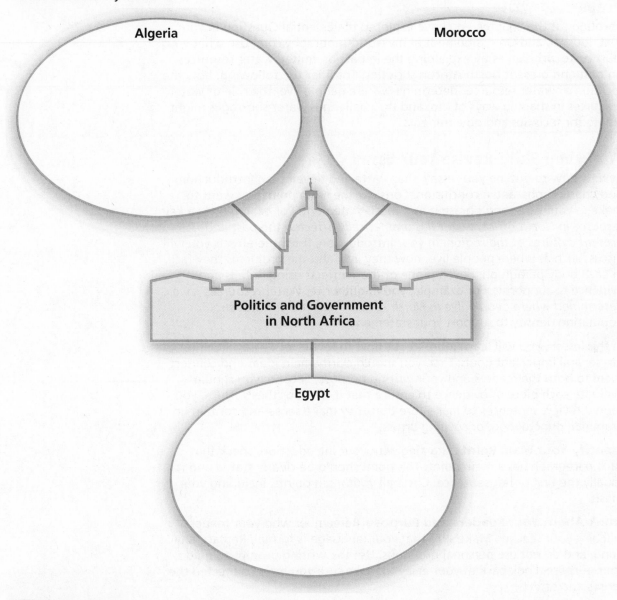

Algeria

Morocco

Politics and Government
in North Africa

Egypt

Essential Question

How has oil affected life in North Africa today?

_____

_____

_____

Essential Question Writer's Workshop

How much does geography shape a country?

Prepare to Write

Throughout this chapter, you have explored the Essential Question in your text, journal, and On Assignment at myWorldGeography.com. Use what you learned to write an essay explaining the impact of limited water resources on past and present North African societies. Consider the following: how the location of water resources determines where people live; the role of water resources in shaping ways of life; and the challenges water shortages might create for societies and governments.

Workshop Skill: Revise Your Essay

Review how to outline your essay, then write and develop an introduction, body paragraphs, and a conclusion. Consider the main point you want to make in your essay and phrase it as a thesis statement. For example: *As a key resource in North Africa, water has dramatically affected the past and present cultures of the region.* In your introduction, list three effects you will discuss such as where people live, how they live, and the problems they face. In each body paragraph, develop one of these effects using details and evidence to support it. For example, you might write, *Water resources have determined where people live in North Africa.* Then provide statistics for population density to support your statement.

In this lesson, you will learn more about how to revise your essay. Revision has several important goals: First, you should clarify main ideas and connect them to both the readers and your writing purpose. Second, you should evaluate each piece of evidence to ensure that it fits your thesis. Third, you should review sentences to make sure that they make sense and contain no grammar, punctuation, or spelling errors.

Identify Your Main Points Starting with your introduction, check that each paragraph has a main point. This point should be clearly stated and is usually the first or last sentence. Circle all your main points, including your thesis.

Think About Your Readers and Purpose Remember who your reader will be—your teacher. Make sure that your language is formal. Replace any slang, and do not use personal pronouns. Use the writing prompt to guide your purpose. Look back at your essay to make sure you have connected the causes and effects.

Evaluate Your Evidence Reread each circled main point. Then carefully read the rest of the paragraph. Does the evidence support the main point? Is the evidence organized in a logical manner? For instance, you might want to list examples from history in chronological order. Also make sure the evidence supports your thesis. You may need to reword your thesis slightly to fit the points you've made. Sentences that don't support the thesis and main ideas should be eliminated.

Be Clear and Correct Now read your essay aloud. Never skip this step! Hearing your sentences will help you notice when they don't flow or if they don't make sense. Ask yourself what you meant to say and use that restatement to rewrite confusing sentences. Then reread silently or use a computer grammar and spelling checker to find and correct any errors.

Here is a sample edited paragraph. The notes in parentheses explain the major revisions:

The location of water in North Africa has long influenced where

people live. For example, ancient Egyptians built their civilization in the

Nile River Valley, which gave them access to the river's water for many

uses. Yearly floods made the soil rich for agriculture, and the river offered

transportation. ~~Work on the river also helped to shape a strong central~~
(not related to the main point)
~~government.~~ About half of today's North Africans still live in Egypt, and
                                        (informal)
almost all of them live near the Nile River. ~~That's~~ They want to be where

the water is. Many other North Africans live along the coast of the

Mediterranean Sea. Nomads travel the deserts and stop at oases to access

water. Each of these population centers have grown due to the need for
(clarifies cause and effect relationship)
water.

Revise Your Essay
Now look critically at one paragraph from your essay and make revisions to improve it. Write your corrected paragraph below.

_____

_____

_____

_____

_____

Draft Your Essay
Copy the revised paragraph into your essay. Use it as a guide in revising the remaining paragraphs. Make sure to check each paragraph for a main idea, supporting evidence, and appropriate spelling, grammar, and punctuation.

? Essential Question

How much does geography shape a country?

Preview Before you begin this chapter, think about the Essential Question. Understanding how the Essential Question connects to your life will help you understand the chapter you are about to read.

Connect to Your Life

(1) What are some ways in which geography shapes your life? Think about how you are influenced by climate, geographic events, or a shortage of resources in your community. Also consider location issues such as urban density or geographic isolation, or economic impacts such as tourism to geographic points of interest. Fill in the table with your responses.

Personal Influence of Geographic Elements				
Parks, Lakes, Rivers	• Local Weather	• Local Crops	• Size of School	• Recreational Activities

(2) How would your family's life change if you lived in a different location?

_____

_____

Connect to the Chapter

(3) Before you read the chapter, flip through every page and note the headings, maps, and pictures. Think about ways that geography's impact on families and communities applies to nations as well. List your ideas in the table below.

Influences of Geographic Elements on a Country				
Physical Features	• Climate	• Natural Resources	• Population	• Culture

(4) After you read the chapter, return to this page. Which of your predictions was inaccurate? Explain why they were wrong.

_____

_____

Name _____ Class _____ Date _____

Connect to myStory:
Hanan's Call to Care

1 Think about ways in which your life is like Hanan's life. What are your cultural beliefs? Have you ever wanted to do something that is unusual in your family or community? Explain.

_____

_____

_____

2 Use this Venn diagram to compare your life with Hanan's life. Think about daily life, plans for the future, and expectations of family and community.

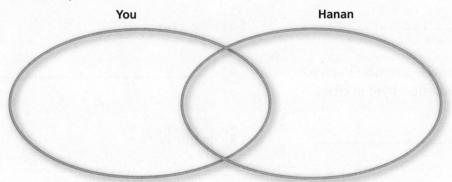

You   Hanan

3 List the challenges that Hanan faces as she tries to plan her future in the table below.

Cultural Rules	Geographic Limits	Political Situations

4 How do you think these challenges affect the citizens in the nations of Arabia and Iraq?

_____

_____

_____

213

Word Wise

Vocabulary Quiz Show Some quiz shows ask a question and expect the contestant to give the answer. In other shows, the contestant is given an answer and must supply the question. If the blank is in the question column, write the question that would result in the answer given. If the question is supplied, write the appropriate answer.

QUESTION

ANSWER

1 _____

1 desalinization

2 What do you call the large pieces of Earth's crust?

2 _____

3 _____

3 fossil fuel

4 What word describes a nation in which most of the population lives in cities?

4 _____

5 _____

5 majority

Name _____ Class _____ Date _____

Take Notes

Map Skills Use the maps in your book to make a key and to label the Places to Know on the outline map below.

Places to Know!

Physical Features	Countries	Cities
Tigris River	Iraq	Baghdad
Euphrates River	United Arab Emirates	Riyadh
Syrian Desert	Yemen	Mecca
Rub'al Khali		
Persian Gulf		
Red Sea		

KEY

0 ___ 200 mi
0 ___ 200 km
Lambert Conformal
Conic Projection

Essential Question

What features of Arabia and Iraq depend on the region's geography?
What features do not depend on its geography?

_____

_____

215

Name _____ Class _____ Date _____

Word Wise

Crossword Puzzle The clues describe key terms from this section. Fill in the numbered *Across* boxes with the correct key terms. Then, do the same with the *Down* clues.

Across	Down
1. a Muslim house of worship	4. worshipping only one god
2. a culture that has writing and where people do many different types of jobs	5. the holy book of Islam
3. a group with less than half of the population	6. an all-powerful leader who has complete control over a nation
	7. an Islamic political and religious leader

Name _____ Class _____ Date _____

Take Notes

Summarize Use what you have read about the history of Arabia and Iraq to complete the table below. In each column, list the main ideas about the topic.

Early Civilizations	Birth of Islam	Muslim Culture	Modern Life

Essential Question

How has geography shaped the history of Arabia and Iraq?
Are there parts of its history that did not depend on its geography?

_____

_____

_____

Word Wise

Words In Context For each question below, write an answer that shows your understanding of the boldfaced key term.

(1) Why do most Muslims in Arabia and Iraq reject **terrorism**?

_____

_____

(2) What is **fundamentalism**?

_____

_____

(3) Why does economic growth depend partly on **entrepreneurship**?

_____

_____

(4) Why do women wear **hijab** in some parts of the Arab world?

_____

_____

(5) How has the concept of **jihad** caused problems for Westerners in the Arab world?

_____

_____

(6) What effect does **Islamism** have on politics and society?

_____

_____

Name _____ Class _____ Date _____

Take Notes

Cause and Effect Use what you read about life in Arabia and Iraq today to complete the table below. In the left column, list at least three factors that have strong influences on life in the region. In the right column, fill in the effect of those influences.

Influences	Effects

Essential Question

What are some challenges the region's nations could face if oil and gas reserves run out?

_____

_____

_____

How much does geography shape a country?

Prepare to Write

Throughout this chapter, you have explored the Essential Question in your text, journal, and On Assignment at myWorldGeography.com. Use what you've learned about Arabia and Iraq to write a persuasive essay in response to this question: Do Arabia's and Iraq's past and present circumstances result mainly from geography or from other factors?

Workshop Skill: Understand the Four Types of Essays

One of the most challenging types of essays to write is the persuasive essay because it expresses an opinion and strives to get readers to agree. The opinion is the essay's "thesis," and it must be stated in the introduction. Remember there is no incorrect opinion; what is important is to thoroughly support your view position.

Write a Thesis Statement First, decide your answer to the question posed. Do you think that the region's past and present circumstances result mainly from geography or from other factors? If you think it was other factors, identify them. Then write a complete sentence expressing your idea. Include the key words from the question in your answer. Here's an example:

Culture, more than geography, has determined the past and present circumstances in Arabia and Iraq.

Your thesis statement _____

_____

Write an Introduction Your thesis must reflect the essay's main arguments. Think of a logical way to organize three important arguments that support your opinion. In this case, time is a good way to organize ideas. Notice how this mini-outline states arguments in historical sequence. Each also shows a cause-and-effect relationship that answers the prompt question.

Reason One Early civilizations in the region created the model for later cultures.

Reason Two The religion of Islam became both the main cultural influence and the main cause of dissent in the region.

Reason Three Conflicts between traditional and modern cultures led to current ways of life and conflicts.

Organize Your Essay

Like all essays, the persuasive essay will have an introduction, three body paragraphs, and a conclusion. Organize your essay following the model shown here.

Paragraph 1: Introduction Remember to open with a catchy question or statement, known as a "hook" to get readers interested. Expand your thesis statement to suggest the three arguments you listed.

Paragraph 2: First Body Paragraph State your first argument and use at least two details to support it.

Topic sentence *Early civilizations in the region created models for later cultures.*
Detail 1 *Assyria became the model for a later Persian empire.*

Detail 2 _____

Concluding Sentence *These early influences remained important as time went on.*

Paragraph 3: Second Body Paragraph Explain your second argument. In the example, notice how time order transition words help the reader move into this new paragraph.

Topic Sentence *In the 600s, the new religion of Islam began to shape*

_____

Detail 1 _____

Detail 2 _____

Concluding Sentence _____

Paragraph 4: Third Body Paragraph Explan your third argument. Add detail to the topic sentence given below and use a time order transition to move from the previous paragraph.

Topic Sentence *Even today,* _____

Detail 1 _____

Detail 2 _____

Concluding Sentence _____

Paragraph 5: Conclusion In the conclusion, summarize the main arguments that support your thesis. End by relating your opinion to a current event or a probable future event.

_____

To interact successfully with the people in the Arabian region, people

around the world must _____

Draft Your Essay

Write your essay on another sheet of paper. When you're done, proofread it with a partner.

Name _____ Class _____ Date _____

Is conflict unavoidable?

Preview Before you begin this chapter, think about the Essential Question. Understanding how the Essential Question connects to your life will help you understand the chapter you are about to read.

Connect to Your Life

① What has caused conflicts in your family, school, community, or state? Name two recent conflicts.

_____

② Listed in the table below are three reasons that conflicts begin. Rate how likely each one is to cause conflict, with 1 being likely and 5 being unlikely. To help decide, you may want to consider the conflicts you named.

Reason for Conflict	How likely is it to cause conflict?				
Misunderstandings	1	2	3	4	5
Power struggles	1	2	3	4	5
Differences	1	2	3	4	5
Other: _____	1	2	3	4	5

Connect to the Chapter

③ Preview the chapter by skimming the headings, photographs, and graphics. Predict sources of conflict in the region in the web below. Color-code the conflicts as avoidable or unavoidable. For example, red might be avoidable and green unavoidable.

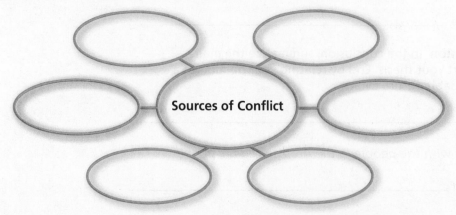

④ After reading the chapter, circle your predictions that were correct.

Name _____ Class _____ Date _____

Connect to myStory: Maayan and Muhammad

① Think about a person or group of people who live in this country but who are unfamiliar to you. Are you afraid of these people? Do they make you feel uneasy? Is it because you do not know very much about them?

_____

_____

_____

② Maayan and Muhammad live in the same nation yet feel apart from each other. Fill in the Venn diagram below to compare Maayan's life with Muhammad's. Think about their families, schools, and concerns.

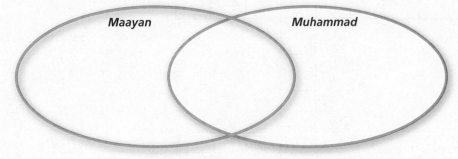

Maayan   *Muhammad*

③ Think about the concerns Maayan and Muhammad mention in their lives. What does this tell you about life in Israel today?

_____

_____

_____

223

Word Wise

Crossword Puzzle The clues describe key terms from this section. Fill in the numbered *Across* with the correct key terms. Then, do the same with the *Down* clues.

Across	Down
1. wells tap into these underground water sources	4. crops thrive in this area that stretches from the Mediterranean coast to the Persian Gulf
2. a member of a religion that combines others teachings with Islam	5. a kind of Islam similar to Shia Islam
3. the dry area on the opposite side of the mountains where the precipitation falls	

Name _____ Class _____ Date _____

Take Notes

Map Skills Use the maps in your book to make a key and to label the Places to Know on the outline map below.

Places to Know!

Physical Features	Territories	Countries	City
Lebanon Mountains	Gaza Strip	Israel	Jerusalem
Syrian Desert	West Bank	Lebanon	
Euphrates River		Syria	
Jordan River		Jordan	
Mediterranean Sea			

N
W E
S

KEY

0   100 mi

0   100 km

Lambert Conformal Conic Projection

Essential Question

Describe steps that Israel and its neighbors have taken to reduce conflict over water resources.

_____

_____

_____

Word Wise

Words In Context For each question below, write an answer that shows your understanding of the boldfaced key term.

1 What did Moses do that showed he was a **prophet**?

_____

_____

2 How do **ethics** help Jews make choices in daily life?

_____

_____

3 Why do Christians believe that the resurrection proves Jesus was a **messiah**?

_____

_____

4 How does the **Trinity** separate Christianity from Judaism and Islam?

_____

_____

5 What did the men fighting in the **Crusades** want to accomplish?

_____

_____

6 How did **agriculture** change the way people lived?

_____

_____

7 What were the goals of **Zionism**?

_____

_____

8 Why did **anti-Semitism** lead millions of Jews to leave Europe?

_____

_____

Name _____ Class _____ Date _____

Take Notes

Compare and Contrast Use what you have read about the history of Israel and its neighbors to complete the table with important events and beliefs from each era.

Jewish Era	Christian Era	Muslim Era	Modern Era
Events:	Events:	Events:	Events:
Beliefs:	Beliefs:	Beliefs:	Beliefs:

Essential Question

Give an example of a conflict in the region. Could it be avoided? If so, explain how.

_____

_____

_____

Word Wise

Vocabulary Quiz Show Some quiz shows ask a question and expect the contestant to give the answer. In other shows, the contestant is given an answer and must supply the question. If the blank is in the question column, write the question that would result in the answer given. If the question is supplied, write the appropriate answer.

QUESTION

ANSWER

① What do you call the areas where Israelis built homes in the Palestinian Territories during the 1970s and 1980s?

① _____

② _____

② capital

③ What is the type of government in which an elected parliament selects the prime minister?

③ _____

④ _____

④ autocracy

⑤ What is the name for a government in which a powerful king passes leadership to his son?

⑤ _____

⑥ _____

⑥ Intifada

Name _____ Class _____ Date _____

Take Notes

Summarize Use what you have read about Israel and its neighbors
to complete the table below. For each topic give details and then write
a one-sentence summary. At the bottom, write a three-sentence overall
summary about the region.

Region's Different Political Systems	Standard of Living
Details:	Details:
Summary:	Summary:
Palestinian-Israeli Conflict	**Region's Global Importance**
Details:	Details:
Summary:	Summary:

Overall Summary:

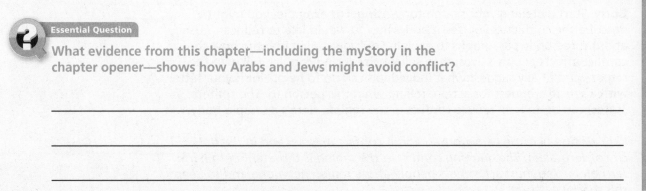

Essential Question

What evidence from this chapter—including the myStory in the
chapter opener—shows how Arabs and Jews might avoid conflict?

_____

_____

_____

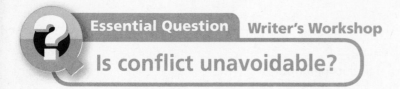

Name _____ Class _____ Date _____

Prepare to Write

Throughout this chapter, you have explored the Essential Question in your text, journal, and On Assignment at myWorldGeography.com. Now you will write a formal letter to answer the question, "How can conflict be reduced or eliminated in this region?"

Workshop Skill: Write a Letter

First, decide who will receive your letter. You might write a letter to the editor of your local paper, to a politician or official of the United States government, or to a government official in a nation in the area (Israel or one of its neighbors). Your letter will tell the recipient ways in which you think he or she can reduce conflict in the region.

Who will receive your letter? _____

Date, Heading, and Greeting In a formal letter, the heading includes your return address and the date in the upper right corner, and the full name and address of the recipient on the left. Skip a line and write the greeting. Most letters use "Dear" and the recipient's name. Use a title such as *Dr., Mrs.,* or *Senator* followed by the person's last name and a colon. Here is an example:

7 Ingram Hill Road
Canton, KY 42211 U.S.A.
May 24, 2012

Mayor Nir Barkat
Jerusalem Town Hall
1234 Jerusalem Avenue
Jerusalem, Israel

Dear Mayor Barkat:

Body Start by telling your reason for writing. For example, you might describe the conflict as you see it and why you would like to reduce it. Use about three body paragraphs to explain your ideas. First identify how the conflict affects people's lives, then tell why reducing conflict will help the region, and finally suggest what individuals can do to help. Finish your letter with a specific request for action, telling what this person (or the United States) can do to help reduce conflict in the region. Here's a sample body:

I am writing because I am worried about conflict in Israel and in the holy city of Jerusalem. The ongoing conflict in the region is threatening to harm Jerusalem. You must act to help people in the region get along and to keep this special city safe.

Since Jerusalem is important to people of many different religions, I think you should try to build a bridge between religions. You can do this with your personal example. Visit some churches or mosques in Jerusalem. Show that you respect these other faiths and their attachment to the city. You could even start an organization that brings Jewish, Christian, and Muslim religious leaders together. You could also invite some leaders of these communities to be part of the city's government. It would be helpful to get ideas from everyone.

Conclusion, Closing, and Signature Conclude by briefly restating your main point. If you want the recipient to take action, such as working to pass a law or printing your letter in the newspaper, state that. Then skip a line and write a closing such as "Yours truly" followed by a comma. Sign your full name.

Draft Your Letter

Use the format below to write the first draft of your letter.

(your address and date; do not put your name) _____

_____

_____

_____ **(name and address of recipient)**

_____

_____

_____

Dear _____

Body _____

_____

Conclusion _____

_____

Closing _____

Your signature _____

Finalize Your Letter

Congratulations! You have drafted a formal letter. Remember to follow the steps of the writing process to revise and edit it. Proofread carefully to ensure all the spelling, punctuation, and grammar are correct. Then neatly copy the letter onto a clean sheet of paper.

Essential Question

What are the challenges of diversity?

Preview Before you begin this chapter, think about the Essential Question. Understanding how the Essential Question connects to your life will help you understand the chapter you are about to read.

Connect to Your Life

(1) Think about a time when you learned about a new culture. Name two ways in which the culture differed from your own.

_____

_____

(2) Think about how there is a wide range of differences in the likes and dislikes of a group of people. Think about some general ways in which people express their differences in taste. Fill in the table below with your ideas.

Categories	Clothing	Food	Music	Interests
Expressions of Different Taste				

Connect to the Chapter

(3) Preview the chapter by skimming the chapter's headings, photographs, and graphics. In the table below, predict the kind of challenges that diversity might present to the people of Iran, Turkey, and Cyprus. An example is given in the ethnic category. Fill in a prediction of your own in each of the other columns.

Types of Diversity	Ethnic	Religious	Political	Linguistic
Challenges	People from different ethnic groups may have different traditions and gender roles.			

(4) After you read the chapter, return to your predictions above. Did anything you learned about diversity in Iran, Turkey, and Cyprus surprise you? Explain.

_____

_____

Connect to myStory: Bilal Looks Forward

① Do you identify with a specific ethnic group? Why or why not?

_____

_____

_____

② List four facts about the Kurds that you learned from reading Bilal's story.

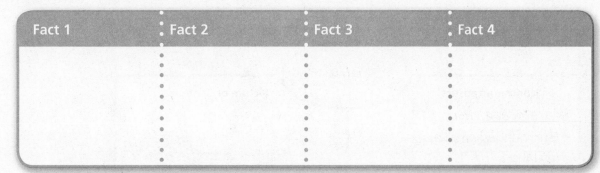

Fact 1	Fact 2	Fact 3	Fact 4

③ How do your career goals compare to Bilal's?

_____

_____

_____

④ What does Bilal's story tell you about life in Turkey today?

_____

_____

_____

Word Wise

Word Map Follow the model below to make a word map. The key term *strait* is in the center oval. Write the definition in your own words at the upper left. In the upper right, list Characteristics, which means words or phrases that relate to the term. At the lower left list Noncharacteristics, which means words and phrases that would not be associated with it. In the lower right, draw a picture of the key term or use it in a sentence.

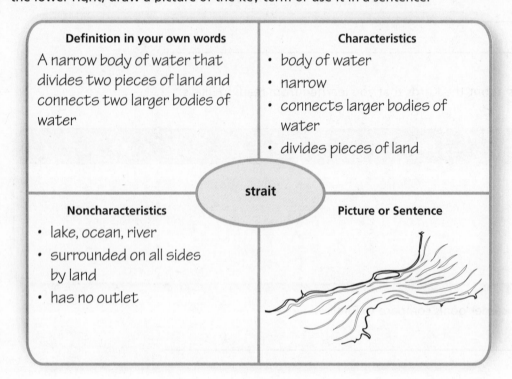

Definition in your own words	**Characteristics**
A narrow body of water that divides two pieces of land and connects two larger bodies of water	• body of water • narrow • connects larger bodies of water • divides pieces of land
Noncharacteristics	**Picture or Sentence**
• lake, ocean, river • surrounded on all sides by land • has no outlet	

(center oval: strait)

Now use the word map below to explore the meaning of the word *shamal*. You may use your student text, a dictionary, and/or a thesaurus to complete each of the four sections.

Definition in your own words	**Characteristics**
Noncharacteristics	**Picture or Sentence**

(center oval: shamal)

Make word maps of your own on a separate piece of paper for these words: *qanat* and *Zoroastrianism*.

Name _____ Class _____ Date _____

Take Notes

Map Skills Use the maps in your book to make a key and to label the Places to Know on the outline map below.

Places to Know!

Physical Features	Cities	Countries
Black Sea	Nicosia	Turkey
Zagros Mountains	Istanbul	Iran
Taurus Mountains	Tehran	Cyprus
Anatolian Plateau		

```
                    N
              W --+-- E
                    S
```

KEY

```
0            200 mi
0    200 km
Lambert Conformal Conic Projection
```

Essential Question

What political issues have arisen from the ethnic diversity of these countries?

_____

_____

_____

235

Word Wise

Sentence Builder Complete the sentences using the information you learned in this section. Include terminal punctuation.

① Persian emperors sent **satraps** to _____

_____

② A **shah** is similar to a king because he _____

_____

③ When people talk about the **Armenian Genocide**, they are referring to

_____

④ People can assume that an **Ayatollah** _____

_____

⑤ The Ottomans used **millets** to organize _____

_____

⑥ Mustafa Kemal was known as **Ataturk** because _____

_____

Name _____ Class _____ Date _____

Take Notes

Sequence Use what you have read about the history of Iran and Turkey to complete the timeline. Next to each event that you list, write an *I* (for Iran) or a *T* (for Turkey).

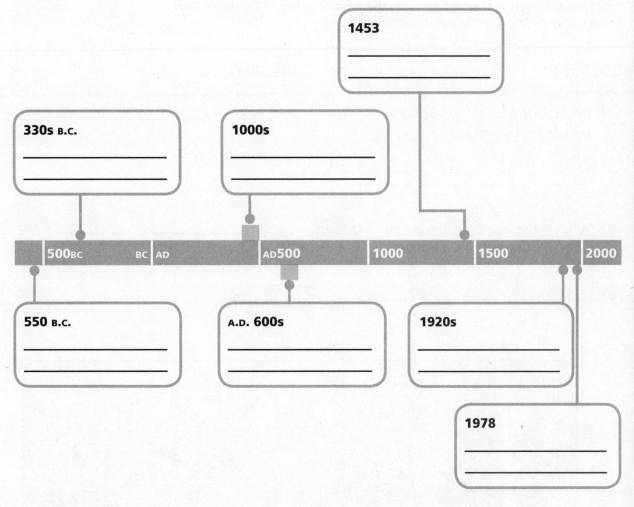

1453
_____
_____

330s B.C.
_____
_____

1000s
_____
_____

550 B.C.
_____
_____

A.D. 600s
_____
_____

1920s
_____
_____

1978
_____
_____

500BC   BC | AD   AD500   1000   1500   2000

Essential Question

What role did national feeling play in the creation of modern Turkey and Iran?

_____

_____

_____

Word Wise

Vocabulary Quiz Show Some quiz shows ask a question and expect the contestant to give the answer. In other shows, the contestant is given an answer and must supply the question. If the blank is in the question column, write the question that would result in the answer given. If the question is supplied, write the appropriate answer.

QUESTION

ANSWER

1. What do you call it when many educated people leave a country?

1. _____

2. _____

2. Majlis

3. What is the name for the religious leaders on Iran's Council of Guardians?

3. _____

4. _____

4. coup

Name _____ Class _____ Date _____

Take Notes

Main Ideas and Details Today Iran, Turkey, and Cyprus each face major challenges. For each issue listed, describe the main idea. Then give two details that tell more about the main idea.

Challenges Facing Iran, Turkey, and Cyprus		
Iran	Turkey	Cyprus
Citizens' Rights: Details:	Secular Democracy: Details:	History of Division: Details:
Role in the World: Details:	Culture: Details:	Events of 1974: Details:
Economy: Details:	Economy: Details:	Current Situation: Details:

? Essential Question

What political conflict has arisen in Turkey as a result of different views about religion?

_____

_____

_____

What are the challenges of diversity?

Prepare to Write

Throughout this chapter, you have explored the Essential Question in your text, journal, and On Assignment at myWorldGeography.com. Use what you've learned to write an essay describing the challenges diversity presents for one of these nations: Iran, Turkey, or Cyprus. Make sure you thoroughly describe the diversity in your chosen nation. Then, identify specific problems and clearly explain how diversity has caused or contributed to those problems.

Workshop Skill: Use the Writing Process

Writing is a bit like a board game. Sometimes you go forward a step and sometimes you have to move backwards a few steps. In the writing process, you complete four basic steps. Yet sometimes you must repeat some of them along the way.

In this lesson, you will learn about the four basic steps in writing an essay. The steps are prewriting, drafting, revising, and presenting. Each step has several parts that help you to communicate your ideas effectively.

Prewrite This step includes everything you do before you start writing. First, choose a country. Then, brainstorm about the challenges of diversity in that country. You might scan chapter headings and images or talk with a partner to get ideas. Collect ideas in note form or use a graphic organizer. Next, make an outline. It should list your main idea or thesis and at least three arguments or reasons that will explain your thesis. Return to the chapter and look for evidence—quotes, statistics, examples, etc.—that will support your reasons. Add these to your outline.

Draft Start putting your ideas into sentences and paragraphs. Follow your outline, but don't worry too much about spelling, grammar, or even complete sentences. Just get your ideas onto paper. Mark places where you may need to get more information. Think about how you can explain your ideas to readers. Try to start each paragraph with a topic sentence that communicates its main point. This will help you know what else needs to go in the paragraph.

Revise Read over your draft. Ask yourself if your ideas and explanations make sense. Think about whether "idea A" belongs before or after "idea B." Move text around until the ideas flow. Then read your draft aloud, listening for sentences that ramble on. Shorten them or create two sentences. On the other hand, if you have too many short sentences, combine sentences to keep your writing from sounding choppy. Read your essay a third time to find and fix spelling and grammar errors. While revising, you may find that you need to do more research or write more text.

Present Create a final copy of your essay. Add your name, date, and a title according to the format your teacher has requested.

Here is a simple table used for brainstorming. You may want to refer to the notes you made on page 239 for your nation.

Cyprus	
Type of Diversity	Problem Caused
ethnic	fighting
political	people have been displaced from their homes

Use a Graphic Organizer

Now create and complete your own graphic organizer to brainstorm ideas for your essay. You can use the table style shown above or any other style that helps you to think creatively.

Draft Your Essay

Use the graphic organizer you created to collect ideas for your essay. Then follow the steps in this workshop to draft and revise your essay on a separate piece of paper. Be sure to follow the four steps in the writing process.

Essential Question

What should governments do?

Preview Before you begin this chapter, think about the Essential Question. Understanding how the Essential Question connects to your life will help you understand the chapter you are about to read.

Connect to Your Life

(1) Think of different ways in which the United States government of the affects your life. List at least one way in each column.

How the United States Government Affects My Life				
Laws	• Taxes	• Military	• Environment	• Transportation
	•	•	•	•
	•	•	•	•
	•	•	•	•
	•	•	•	•
	•	•	•	•

Connect to the Chapter

(2) Think about some of the bad times that countries go through, such as wars or economic slowdowns. In the Venn diagram below, list at least something a government should do during bad times, and something it should do during good times. In the intersection, list what a government should do at *all* times.

What should governments do?

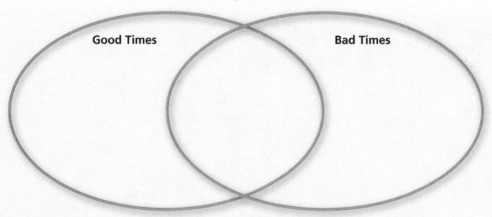

Good Times   Bad Times

(3) Preview the chapter by skimming the chapter's headings, photographs, and graphics. Using a different colored pen or pencil, add to the Venn digram some predictions of how the governments of Central Asia and the Caucasus have acted.

(4) Read the chapter. Put a check mark next to your correct predictions.

Name _____ Class _____ Date _____

Connect to myStory: Askar Serves His People

(1) Name two problems that have affected your neighborhood or region. What caused these problems? Have they been solved?

_____

_____

_____

(2) Are the problems in your area ones that the government can solve? Explain why or why not.

_____

_____

_____

(3) What problems has Askar experienced in his neighborhood? Describe them in the table below.

Water	Electricity	Temperature	School

(4) In the table above, circle the problems which you think the Kyrgyzstan government has the ability to solve.

(5) How do you think these problems affect the people living in Kyrgyzstan?

_____

_____

_____

Word Wise

Vocabulary Quiz Show Some quiz shows ask a question and expect the contestant to give the answer. In other shows, the contestant is given an answer and must supply the question. If the blank is in the question column, write the question that would result in the answer given. If the question is supplied, write the appropriate answer.

QUESTION	ANSWER
(1) What do you call a nation that is cut off from direct contact with the oceans?	(1) _____
(2) _____	(2) irrigate
(3) What term describes herd animals eating so much grass that the plants cannot recover?	(3) _____
(4) _____	(4) riot
(5) What do you call Kazakhstan's broad grasslands?	(5) _____
(6) _____	(6) temperate

Name _____ Class _____ Date _____

Take Notes

Map Skills Use the maps in your book to make a key and to label the Places to Know on the outline map below.

Places to Know!	
Physical Features	**Countries**
Caucasus Mountains	Armenia
Caspian Sea	Azerbaijan
Aral Sea	Georgia
Amu Dar'ya River	Kazakhstan
Syr Dar'ya River	Kyrgyzstan
	Uzbekistan

Essential Question

Should the governments of Tajikistan and Kyrgyzstan build hydroelectric dams if the dams will reduce the amount of water that flows to neighboring countries? Explain.

_____

_____

_____

Word Wise

Word Map Follow the model below to make a word map. The key term *merchant* is in the center oval. Write the definition in your own words at the upper left. In the upper right, list Characteristics, which means words or phrases that relate to the term. At the lower left list Noncharacteristics, which means words and phrases that would not be associated with it. In the lower right, draw a picture of the key term or use it in a sentence.

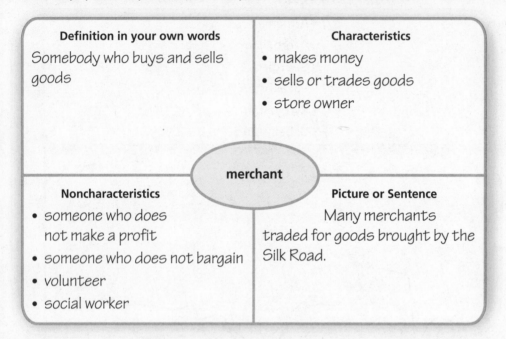

Definition in your own words
Somebody who buys and sells goods

Characteristics
- makes money
- sells or trades goods
- store owner

merchant

Noncharacteristics
- someone who does not make a profit
- someone who does not bargain
- volunteer
- social worker

Picture or Sentence
Many merchants traded for goods brought by the Silk Road.

Now use the word map below to explore the meaning of the word *caravan*. You may use your student text, a dictionary, and/or a thesaurus to complete each of the four sections.

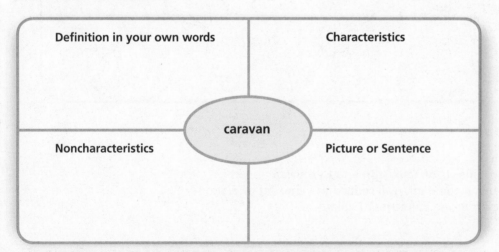

Definition in your own words

Characteristics

caravan

Noncharacteristics

Picture or Sentence

Make word maps of your own on a separate piece of paper for these words: *sedentary*, *Silk Road,* and *madrassa*.

246

Name _____ Class _____ Date _____

Take Notes

Summarize Use what you have read about the history of trade and empires in Central Asia and the Caucasus to complete the concept web below. In the top section, write what you have learned about the history of trade and cultures in the region. In the bottom section, write details about the history of empires in the region.

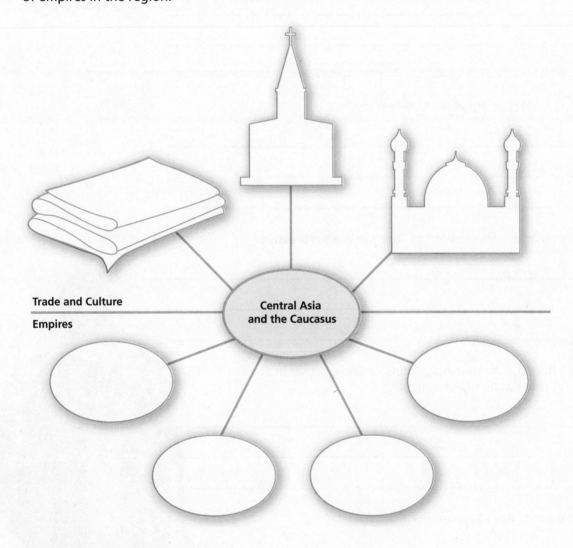

Trade and Culture

Empires

Central Asia
and the Caucasus

Essential Question

Why did the Soviet government encourage the Russian language in this region? Should the government choose the official language of the country?

_____

_____

Word Wise

Words In Context For each question below, write an answer that shows your understanding of the boldfaced key term.

(1) Why has the government of Kyrgyzstan supported the **akyn**?

_____

_____

_____

(2) How does **election fraud** limit democracy?

_____

_____

_____

(3) What makes the government of Turkmenistan **repressive**?

_____

_____

_____

(4) What effect did the **demonstrations** in Georgia that occurred in 2003 have on that nation's government?

_____

_____

_____

(5) What was the **Rose Revolution**?

_____

_____

_____

Name _____ Class _____ Date _____

Take Notes

Main Ideas and Details In the textbook, there are three headings for this
section. They are listed below on the left. Write the main idea from each
part in your own words. Then, for each main idea list at least two supporting
details in the column on the right.

Main Ideas	Supporting Details
Cultural Life of Central Asia and the Caucasus _____ _____ _____	_____ _____ _____ _____ _____
Challenges for New Nations _____ _____ _____	_____ _____ _____ _____
Building New Governments _____ _____ _____	_____ _____ _____ _____

Essential Question

Do you think the governments of Central Asia and the Caucasus
should try to make farmers and businesses reduce pollution?
Explain.

_____

_____

_____

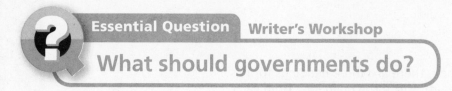

Essential Question Writer's Workshop

What should governments do?

Prepare to Write

Throughout this chapter, you have explored the Essential Question in your text, journal, and On Assignment at myWorldGeography.com. Use what you've learned to write an essay about what governments should do in Central Asia and the Caucasus. Consider some of the actions governments have taken in this region. Also, think about how the role of some of these governments should change.

Workshop Skill: Outline an Essay

Good essays are not only factually correct, they also catch the reader's attention with a "hook." In addition, a well-constructed essay uses a thesis statement to prepare the reader to move through the essay.

The Hook Think about how the governments of Central Asia and the Caucasus have acted since the fall of the Soviet Union. Are there some actions you agree with? Are there some you disagree with? Find three examples. Then create a "hook," one or more sentences that will catch the reader's attention. For example, you could open with: *Imagine if your neighbor cut the water to your house so that just a trickle came from your faucet.* Notice how this statement creates personal interest in the reader. On the lines below, write some hook ideas to generate interest in the fact that how the nations of Kyrgyzstan and Tajikistan have built hydroelectric dams that have reduced the water flow into nearby nations.

_____

_____

The Thesis Statement After the hook, state your thesis, which is the main idea of your essay. Your thesis should state three ideas you will use to support your position. These ideas will be the focus of your three body paragraphs. In this case, the thesis statement is the last sentence in your introduction. Add two of your own ideas to the thesis statement given below.

Example *The governments of Kyrgyzstan and Tajikistan have built*

hydroelectric dams that have reduced the water flow into the nearby nations

of Uzbekistan and Turkmenistan. The action that some of the governments

of Central Asia and the Caucasus have taken concerning water shortage,

_____, and _____ have been controversial

and should change.

Organize Your Essay

Paragraph 1: Introduction Remember the hook ideas? Begin your introductory paragraph with one of those and end it by clearly stating your thesis.

Paragraph 2: Body Paragraph A In your thesis, you stated three ideas about what governments should do. State one of these ideas in Body Paragraph A and use at least two details to support it.

Topic Sentence *The governments of Kyrgyzstan and Tajikistan have supported the building of hydroelectric dams.*

Detail 1 *These dams reduce the flow of water into nearby nations.*

Detail 2 _____

Concluding Sentence *To prevent a water shortage in Uzbekistan and Turkmenistan, the governments of Kyrgyzstan and Tajikistan should prohibit the building of more dams in their own countries.*

Paragraph 3: Body Paragraph B Review your thesis and note your idea for the second topic, which will be the focus of Paragraph B. Try to make a smooth transition as you begin a new paragraph.

Topic Sentence *In addition to preventing water shortages, governments in*

Central Asia and the Caucasus should also _____ .

Detail 1 _____

Detail 2 _____

Concluding Sentence _____

Paragraph 4: Body Paragraph C Follow the steps given for body paragraphs 1 and 2 to write your third body paragraph.

Paragraph 5: Conclusion For the conclusion, summarize the ideas you presented in your thesis.

The examples of water shortage, _____ *, and*

_____ *shows how the roles of some of the governments of*

Central Asia and the Caucasus need to change. By studying the region's

governments, it is clear that _____ .

This shows that governments should _____

and should not _____

Draft Your Essay

Write your essay and then proofread it with a writing partner.

Name _____ Class _____ Date _____

What makes a nation?

Preview Before you begin this chapter, think about the Essential Question. Understanding how the Essential Question connects to your life will help you understand the chapter you are about to read.

Connect to Your Life

① Think of countries that you've learned about from reading or from the news. What made each country unique and different from other countries? Write your ideas in the table below.

Things That Make Nations Different From Each Other			
Institutions	• Geography	• Culture	• Other

② Look at the table. Which categories do you think have the greatest effect on the individual character of a nation?

_____

_____

Connect to the Chapter

③ Now think about setting up a nation from scratch. What are the basic needs of a new nation? In the concept web below, predict factors that played a part in shaping the unique nations of South Asia.

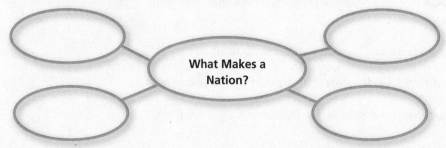

What Makes a Nation?

④ After you read the chapter, return to your predictions above. Would you change any of your responses now? Why or why not?

_____

_____

_____

Name _____ Class _____ Date _____

Connect to myStory:
Nancy's Fruitful Loan

(1) Do you think it's important for teenagers to learn to work cooperatively with other people? Explain.

_____

_____

(2) What has Nancy learned about cooperation from helping her mother at the canning cooperative? Use your ideas to fill in the web below.

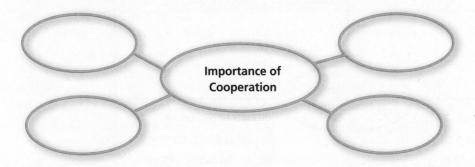

Importance of Cooperation

(3) How important is cooperation to the success or failure of the canning cooperative?

_____

_____

(4) Can cooperation help a nation to function better? How?

_____

_____

Name _____ Class _____ Date _____

Word Wise

Word Map Follow the model below to make a word map. The key
term *Indian subcontinent* is in the center oval. Write the definition in
your own words at the upper left. In the upper right, list Characteristics,
which means words or phrases that relate to the term. At the lower left,
list Noncharacteristics, which means words and phrases that would not
be associated with it. In the lower right, draw a picture of the key term
or use it in a sentence.

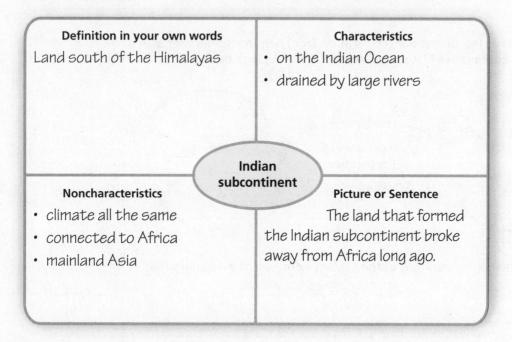

Definition in your own words
Land south of the Himalayas

Characteristics
• on the Indian Ocean
• drained by large rivers

Indian subcontinent

Noncharacteristics
• climate all the same
• connected to Africa
• mainland Asia

Picture or Sentence
The land that formed
the Indian subcontinent broke
away from Africa long ago.

Now use the word map below to explore the meaning of the word *flood
plains*. You may use your student text, a dictionary, and/or a thesaurus to
complete each of the four sections.

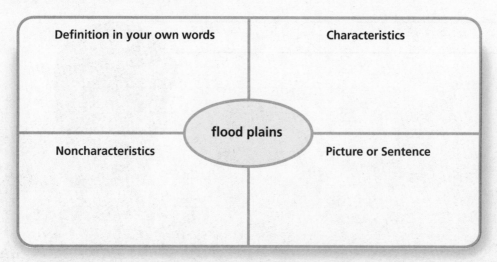

Definition in your own words

Characteristics

flood plains

Noncharacteristics

Picture or Sentence

Make word maps of your own on a separate piece of paper for these key
terms: *Green Revolution* and *subsistence farming*.

254

Name _____ Class _____ Date _____

Take Notes

Map Skills Use the maps in your book to make a key and to label the Places to Know on the outline map below.

Places to Know!

Physical Features		Cities	
Himalayas	Deccan Plateau	Calcutta	Lahore
Ganges River	Thar Desert	Mumbai	Delhi
Indus River	Hindu Kush		

KEY

0 _____ 400 mi
0 _____ 400 km
Lambert Conformal Conic Projection

Essential Question

How does the geography of a nation help create a common bond among its people and help shape its national identity?

_____

_____

_____

Word Wise

Crossword Puzzle The clues describe key terms from this section. Fill in the numbered *Across* boxes with the correct key terms. Then, do the same with the *Down* clues.

Across	Down
1. The _____ system divides society into distinct groups.	5. a policy in which India did not declare itself an ally of either superpower during the Cold War
2. a state of great understanding and freedom	6. the religion of most Indians today
3. to split a country into two nations	7. a place where civilization begins and then spreads
4. the religion that developed from the teachings of Siddhartha Gautama	

Name _____ Class _____ Date _____

Take Notes

Cause and Effect Use what you have read about the history of South Asia to complete the table below. Give the approximate date or time period of each event. Then identify the effects of each event.

Cause	Effect
Traders carry goods from the Indus Valley civilization. Time period:	
Invaders enter the Indian subcontinent and mix with local communities. Time period:	
Ashoka takes control of South Asia after Alexander's retreat. Date:	
Muslim rulers establish the Delhi Sultanate. Time period:	
European traders set up ports. Time period:	
Gandhi heads a movement to force Britain to release its control over India. Time period:	

Essential Question

Do you agree or disagree with Gandhi's and Nehru's idea of a nation?

_____

_____

Word Wise

Vocabulary Quiz Show Some quiz shows ask a question and expect the contestant to give the answer. In other shows, the contestant is given an answer and must supply the question. If the blank is in the question column, write the question that would result in the answer given. If the question is supplied, write the appropriate answer.

QUESTION	ANSWER
(1) What do you call a long poem that tells a story filled with adventure and conflict?	(1) _____
(2) _____	(2) Bollywood
(3) What do call you a representative government that is not based on religion?	(3) _____
(4) _____	(4) outsourcing

Name _____ Class _____ Date _____

Take Notes

Summarize Use what you have read about South Asia today to complete the table below. Write at least two important ideas that sum up each topic.

Culture
1.
2.

Population Growth
1.
2.

Pollution
1.
2.

Religious Conflict
1.
2.

Governments
1.
2.

Economies
1.
2.

Essential Question

What problems threaten the national unity of each nation in South Asia?

_____

_____

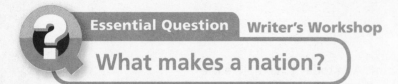

Essential Question Writer's Workshop

What makes a nation?

Prepare to Write

Throughout this chapter, you have explored the Essential Question in your text, journal, and On Assignment at myWorldGeography.com. Use what you've learned to write a essay on how the idea of a nation might differ among the nations in South Asia. Include information about South Asia's varied languages, religions, and cultures. Also keep in mind the effect of invasion and colonization on the nations' development.

Workshop Skill: Write an Introduction and Thesis Statement

Before you begin writing, review some ways to explore the Essential Question by brainstorming, free writing, or creating an idea web. Doing so will help you to figure out your thesis statement, which is the major point of your essay.

In this lesson, you will learn how to write a thesis statement and an introduction. These two parts set up your essay and provide a "road map" for your reader.

Develop a Thesis Statement Use your prewriting ideas to help you draft a thesis statement that identifies the main idea of your essay. Keep in mind that a successful essay supports and expands upon the thesis statement. All the information in your essay should connect to this important idea.

On the one hand, a thesis statement should not be too general. Ask yourself these questions: Is my thesis statement vague? Can I cover this idea in one essay, or would it take a book? For example, this thesis statement is too general: *South Asia is composed of a great variety of nations.*

On the other hand, a thesis statement should not be too specific. Ask yourself these questions: Is my thesis statement narrow? Does it focus on a very limited part of the chapter? Can I write a whole essay on this idea? For example, thesis statement is too specific: *Britain's colonial empire in South Asia affected the kind of nations that developed there.*

Here is an example of a solid thesis statement: *Many influences shaped the languages, cultures, and religions of South Asia and contributed to the kinds of nations that developed there.*

Compose an Introduction The purpose of an introduction is to present your thesis to your readers and to lead into your essay. Your introduction makes a first impression. How can you be sure that it is a good impression? Your introduction has to be interesting. It should make your reader want to read on.

Connect Start with an idea connected to your thesis: *South Asia sits at a geographic crossroads.*

Expand Develop the idea by adding a little detail: *The region is sandwiched between Europe, the Middle East, Asia, and Southeast Asia.*

Explain Let your readers know why this is important: *As a result, South Asia was a natural route and a stopping point for invaders, traders, and travelers.*

Synthesize Now put it all together: *South Asia sits at a geographic crossroads. The region is sandwiched between Europe, the Middle East, Asia, and Southeast Asia. As a result, South Asia was a natural route and a stopping point for invaders, traders, and travelers. These influences shaped the languages, cultures, and religions of South Asia and contributed to the kinds of nations that developed there.*

Write a Thesis Statement and Introduction

Now write your own thesis statement and introduction for your essay.

Thesis Statement _____

_____

Connect _____

_____

Expand _____

_____

Explain _____

_____

Synthesize _____

_____

_____

_____

Draft Your Essay

Write your essay on your own paper using the introduction you just developed. Be sure to include three body paragraphs and a concluding paragraph. When you have finished, proofread your essay with a partner. Then write a final copy.

Name _____ Class _____ Date _____

How can you measure success?

Preview Before you begin this chapter, think about the Essential Question. Understanding how the Essential Question connects to your life will help you understand the chapter you are about to read.

Connect to Your Life

(1) Think of some ways to measure success in the categories shown in the table below. List at least one way to measure success to measure success in each column. For example, under school you could list grades.

Measures of Personal Success			
Family	Friends	School	Other (Sports, Arts, Chores)

(2) Look at the table. Compare the ways to measure success. How are they alike? How are they different?

_____

_____

Connect to the Chapter

(3) Now think about ways to measure a country's success. For instance, pollution levels can measure a country's success with environmental protection. Preview the chapter by skimming the chapter's headings, photographs, and graphics. In the table below, list at least one way to measure China's success in each category. Then predict if China has achieved success in each category. For example, if you think that China has high pollution, it would show a lack of success with the environment.

Measures of National Success			
Economy	Politics	Social Services	Environment

(4) Read the chapter. Then circle your predictions in the table that were correct.

Name _____ Class _____ Date _____

Connect to myStory: Xiao's Lake

Name two changes you have seen in your neighborhood or region. Are these changes good or bad? Explain why.

_____

_____

_____

What changes has Xiao seen in his neighborhood or region? Write them in the table under the correct headings.

Economy	Lake Tai	Government Decisions

How do you think these changes are affecting China? Write at least two predictions.

_____

_____

_____

_____

Word Wise

Vocabulary Quiz Show Some quiz shows ask a question and expect the contestant to give the answer. In other shows, the contestant is given an answer and must supply the question. If the blank is in the question column, write the question that would result in the answer given. If the question is supplied, write the appropriate answer.

QUESTION

ANSWER

1. What do you call a person whose job is to move with animals from place to place during the year?

1. _____

2. _____

2. one-child policy

3. What is the name for the major crop that feeds most people in a region?

3. _____

4. _____

4. loess

5. What do you call the kind of land where crops can be grown?

5. _____

Name _____ Class _____ Date _____

Take Notes

Map Skills Use the maps in your book to make a key and to label the Places to Know on the outline map below.

Places to Know!

Physical Features	Countries	Cities
Huang River	• Mongolia	• Beijing
Chang River	• Taiwan	• Shanghai
North China Plain		
Plateau of Tibet		

N
W — E
S

Yellow
Sea

East
China
Sea

KEY

0 _____ 400 mi

0 _____ 400 km

Lambert Conformal Conic Projection

South
China
Sea

Essential Question

How can the Chinese government measure
whether or not the one-child policy has been successful?

_____

_____

_____

Word Wise

Word Bank Choose one word from the word bank to fill in each blank.
When you have finished, you will have a short summary of important ideas
from the section.

Word Bank

famine	Confucianism
Daoism	command economy
dynasty	

About 3,800 years ago, China was ruled by its first

_____. This was a ruling family where power passed from

one person to another. No one outside this family could lead the nation.

During this time, two belief systems developed. The first, called

_____,was named after its founder, Confucius. He

emphasized that people should follow rules and respect leaders. He also

said that leaders should only lead as long as they looked out for the

best interests of their people. The second belief system was

_____. It was based on "the way" or "the path." The idea

was to live in harmony with nature. The ideas of these belief systems did not

conflict with each other. People followed both.

When the dynasties ended, the Chinese Communist Party (CCP) took

charge of China. It created the _____. In this type of system,

the government has a lot of control. It decides what crops should be grown

and what goods should be made. It assigns people to jobs. People have few

choices. The idea was that everyone would have enough to eat. But the

reality was different. The CCP made some poor decisions. This caused a

period of starvation called a _____.

Take Notes

Main Idea and Details Use what you have read about the history of the region to fill in the graphic organizer below. The label above each pagoda corresponds to a heading in this section of the chapter.

Empires of China and Mongolia

Main Idea

_____

_____

Supporting Details

_____

_____

Important Ideas and Beliefs

Main Idea

_____

_____

Supporting Details

_____

_____

End of Dynasties

Main Idea

_____

_____

Supporting Details

_____

_____

China and Mongolia Under Communism

Main Idea

_____

_____

Supporting Details

_____

_____

Essential Question

Do you think the Qing dynasty was unsuccessful?

_____

_____

_____

Word Wise

Crossword Puzzle The clues describe key terms from this section. Fill in the numbered *Across* boxes with the correct key terms. Then, do the same with the *Down* clues.

Across	Down
1. power generated by water	4. what a worker gets for doing a job
2. China's political system is a _____ state.	5. the average number of years a person will live
3. not able to read and write	

Name _____ Class _____ Date _____

Take Notes

Compare and Contrast Fill in the table below to compare and contrast the politics and economies in China, Mongolia, and Taiwan.

Country	Politics	Economies
China		
Mongolia		
Taiwan		

Essential Question

What is one way that China has been successful? Give evidence from the text and from figures to support your point.

_____

_____

_____

Essential Question Writer's Workshop

How can you measure success?

Prepare to Write

Throughout this chapter, you have explored the Essential Question in your text, journal, and On Assignment at myWorldGeography.com. Use what you've learned to write an essay measuring the success of China. Include the following: the economy, politics, social services, and environment of China. Think about the amount of success achieved by China in each category, and what caused its success or lack of success in each category.

Workshop Skill: Write Body Paragraphs

Review how to outline your essay and write an introduction. Phrase the main point you want to make as a thesis statement. For example, *China has achieved great success in some areas and little success in others.* In your introduction, support your thesis with three ideas.

In this lesson, you will learn how to write the body paragraphs. Each body paragraph should develop one of the ideas you listed in the introduction that supports your thesis statement. Each body paragraph expands on the idea by giving details or evidence.

Write a Topic Sentence Start each paragraph with a topic sentence. A topic sentence must clearly state the main idea of the body paragraph, connect that idea to the essay's thesis, and provide a transition from the previous paragraph.

Support the Topic Sentence With Discussion and Facts After your topic sentence, explain and support your point with discussion and details. Discussion sentences connect and explain your main point and supporting details. Supporting details are the actual facts.

End With a Concluding Sentence Finish your paragraph with a sentence that reflects your topic sentence and pulls together the discussion and details.

Here is a sample body paragraph:

Sample topic sentence *China achieved great economic success when it changed from a command economy to a market economy.*

Supporting discussion *Since this change, China has developed one of the world's largest economies.*

Supporting detail *It stresses manufacturing, technology, and services, with agriculture remaining important.*

Supporting discussion *As the economy continues to grow, many companies have expanded and hired new workers.*

Concluding sentence *Now these companies are producing products that are exported all over the world.*

Write a Body Paragraph

Now write your own body paragraph for your essay.

Topic sentence

_____

_____

Supporting discussion

_____

_____

Supporting detail

_____

_____

Supporting detail

_____

_____

Supporting discussion

_____

_____

Concluding sentence

_____

_____

Draft Your Essay

Use the body paragraph above in your complete essay written on your own paper. Be sure that each of your body paragraphs has a topic sentence, supporting details, and a concluding sentence.

Essential Question

How much does geography shape a country?

Preview Before you begin this chapter, think about the Essential Question. Understanding how the Essential Question connects to your life will help you understand the chapter you are about to read.

Connect to Your Life

1 How have the geographic elements listed in the table below affected your life? List the effects listed in each column. For example, under local weather, list the effects of precipitation or temperature on your life.

Personal Influence of Geographic Elements				
Parks, Lakes, Rivers	Local Weather	Local Crops	School Size	Recreational Activities

2 Do you think geography has had a major impact on your life? Explain.

_____

_____

Connect to the Chapter

3 Preview the chapter by skimming the chapter's heads, photographs, and graphics. In the table below, make predictions about how geographic elements affect Japan and the Koreas. For example, you might predict that South Korea's moist, hot climate enables it to grow rice.

Influences of Geographic Elements on Japan and the Koreas				
Physical Features	Climate	Natural Resources	Population	Culture

4 After you have read the chapter, review the predictions you listed. Put a check mark next to ones that were wrong. Why were they incorrect?

_____

_____

_____

Name _____ Class _____ Date _____

Connect to myStory: Asuka: A Girl on the Go

(1) Name at least three ways in which Asuka's life is like your own.

_____

_____

_____

(2) Now think about the ways in which Asuka's life is different from your own. In the table below, record at least three differences. Then circle whether these differences are better or worse. In the third column, tell why you think they are better or worse. An example is given for you.

How Asuka's Life Compares to Mine		
Difference	Compares to Mine	Why?
She has two pets.	(Better) Worse	I've always wanted a pet, but my mom won't let me have one.
	Better Worse	
	Better Worse	
	Better Worse	

(3) What does Asuka's story tell you about life in Japan?

_____

_____

_____

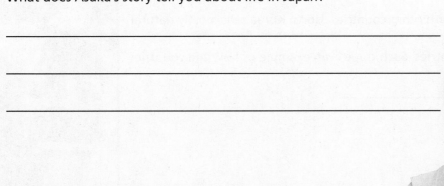

Word Wise

Word Bank Choose one word from the word bank to fill in each blank. When you have finished, you will have a short summary of important ideas from the section.

Word Bank

foliage   scarcity

interdependent   comparative advantage

The Korean peninsula consists largely of hills and mountains. In the

past, forests covered these hills and mountains. Extensive logging has

reduced these forests quite a bit, which has led to mudslides in the rainy

season. However, the fall months are marked, especially in North Korea, by

brilliant displays of _____ as the leaves on the trees in the

forests change color.

Because so much of the Korean peninsula consists of hills and

mountains, there is a _____ of flat land good for farming.

This shortage means that other countries with more farmland have a(n)

_____ over the Koreas. Both Koreas must import some of

their food supplies from other countries. To pay for these imports, the

Koreas trade with other countries. South Korea trades an array of advanced

manufactured goods with other countries. North Korea sells mostly natural

resources to other countries. Such trade is an example of how the countries

of the world are _____.

274

Name _____ Class _____ Date _____

Take Notes

Map Skills Use the maps in your book to make a key and to label the Places to Know on the outline map below.

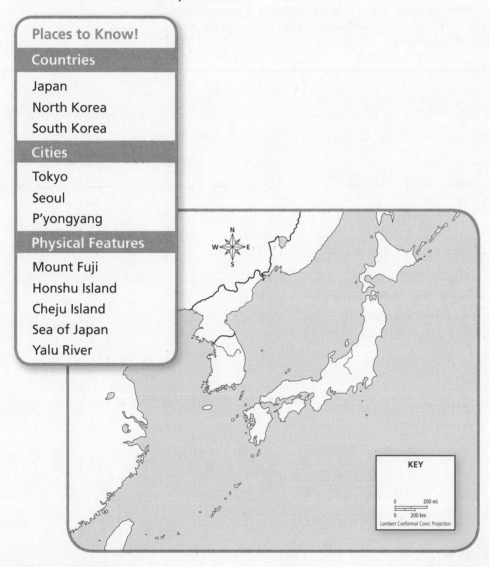

Places to Know!

Countries

Japan

North Korea

South Korea

Cities

Tokyo

Seoul

P'yongyang

Physical Features

Mount Fuji

Honshu Island

Cheju Island

Sea of Japan

Yalu River

KEY

0   200 mi

0   200 km

Lambert Conformal Conic Projection

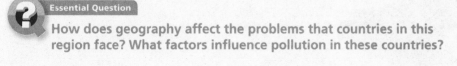

Essential Question

How does geography affect the problems that countries in this region face? What factors influence pollution in these countries?

_____

_____

_____

_____

Word Wise

Vocabulary Quiz Show Some quiz shows ask a question and expect the contestant to give the answer. In other shows, the contestant is given an answer and must supply the question. If the blank is in the question column, write the question that would result in the answer given. If the question is supplied, write the appropriate answer.

QUESTION

ANSWER

1 _____

1 samurai

2 What conflict ended in 1953 without either side winning?

2 _____

3 _____

3 shogun

4 What was the period in the 1800s during which Japan's new leaders wanted to expand their nation's industries and military?

4 _____

5 _____

5 constitutional monarchy

Name _____ Class _____ Date _____

Take Notes

Main Idea and Details In your textbook there are three major headings in this section. They are listed below. Write the main idea from each section in your own words. Then, write at least three supporting details for each section.

Main Idea	Supporting Details
Historical Roots	
_____	_____
_____	_____
_____	_____
	_____
	_____
International Conflicts and Connections	
_____	_____
_____	_____
_____	_____
	_____
	_____
Japan and Koreas Since World War II	
_____	_____
_____	_____
_____	_____
	_____
	_____

Essential Question

Both Japan and Korea chose to limit contact with outsiders at certain times during their histories. How do you think their geography helped them to do that?

_____

_____

_____

Name _____ Class _____ Date _____

Word Wise

Words In Context For each question below, write an answer that shows your understanding of the boldfaced key term.

(1) Why is South Korea's government considered a **limited government**?

_____

_____

_____

(2) Why is North Korea's government considered an **unlimited government**?

_____

_____

_____

(3) What makes Kim Jong-il a **dictator**?

_____

_____

_____

(4) What were some of the effects caused by Japan's **recession** during the 1990s?

_____

_____

_____

(5) What gods or spirits are worshiped in the **Shinto** religion?

_____

_____

_____

Name _____ Class _____ Date _____

Take Notes

Summarize Use what you have read about Japan and the Koreas today to fill in the table below about the economy and daily life and culture in the three countries.

	South Korea	North Korea	Japan
Economy			
Daily Life and Culture			

Essential Question

How important is geography to the differences between North Korea and South Korea?

_____

_____

_____

Name _____ Class _____ Date _____

Writer's Workshop

How much does geography shape a country?

Prepare to Write

Throughout this chapter, you have explored the Essential Question in your text, journal, and On Assignment at myWorldGeography.com. Use what you've learned to write an essay about how geography has shaped Japan or South Korea. Consider the physical features, climate, land use, natural resources, and culture of Japan or South Korea.

Workshop Skill: Write a Conclusion

Review how to outline your essay. Then write an introduction and three body paragraphs on how geography has shaped Japan or South Korea. Be sure to include a thesis statement for the introduction and three or more supporting points in your body paragraphs.

In this lesson, you will learn more about writing the conclusion of your essay. A strong conclusion should tie together the different strands of your essay. It should give your reader the feeling that everything adds up and makes sense. First, you should restate your topic. Then, briefly summarize the points you made in the essay. After this, you should write a few sentences in which you restate your thesis in a new way. End the conclusion by pointing out the importance of the information presented in the essay.

Write a Topic Statement Start your conclusion by restating your topic. The topic statement should convey the main idea of the essay and provide a transition to your summary points. The examples given will be for North Korea.

Sample Topic Sentence: *Geography has shaped North Korea in many ways.*

Support the Topic Sentence With Summary Points After the topic sentence, write two or three sentences that summarize the main points of your body paragraphs. These sentences should not include minor details.

Summary Point *Its lack of farmland has contributed to widespread famine and the death of millions.*

Summary Point *In addition, its mountainous terrain limits the amount of living space.*

Summary Point *However, North Korea's plentiful natural resources have enabled the country to build a strong military and industrial base.*

Restate Your Thesis Next, restate your thesis statement in a way that is different from how you wrote it in the introduction. Doing this will add more emphasis to the thesis.

Sample of Thesis Restatement *As can be seen, the geography of North Korea has strongly affected the way its people live.*

End With a Concluding Sentence Finish your conclusion with a statement that stresses the importance of the information presented in the essay.

Sample Concluding Sentence *Indeed, geography has helped make North Korea the poor and dangerously unstable nation it is today.*

Write Your Conclusion

Now write your own essay's conclusion. Be sure that your conclusion has a topic sentence, summary points, a restatement of the thesis, and a concluding sentence.

Topic Sentence _____

_____

Summary Point _____

_____

Summary Point _____

_____

Summary Point _____

_____

Restate Your Thesis _____

_____

Concluding Sentence _____

_____

Draft Your Essay

Use the conclusion you just created in your complete five-paragraph essay written on your own piece of paper.

Name _____ Class _____ Date _____

What are the challenges of diversity?

Preview Before you begin this chapter, think about the Essential Question. Understanding how the Essential Question connects to your life will help you understand the chapter you are about to read.

Connect to Your Life

1. Think about how there is a wide range of differences in the likes and dislikes of a group of people. For example, you may like hip-hop music while a friend prefers classic rock. Think about some general ways in which people express their differences in taste. Fill in the table below with your ideas.

Categories	Clothing	Food	Music	Interests
Expressions of Different Taste				

2. Do some differences in taste encourage or discourage interaction with other groups? Explain.

_____

_____

Connect to the Chapter

3. Preview the chapter by skimming the chapter's headings, photographs, and graphics. In the table below, predict the kind of challenges that diversity might present to the people of Southeast Asia. An example is given in the religious category. Fill in a prediction of your own in each of the other columns.

Diversity	Ethnic	Religious	Political	Linguistic
Challenges		When people do not share the same religion, they have may have trouble accepting each other's faith.		

4. After you read the chapter, return to this page. Circle your predictions that were accurate.

Name _____ Class _____ Date _____

Connect to myStory:
A Minangkabau Wedding

(1) How is a Minangkabau wedding similar to weddings you have attended or seen on television? How is it different?

_____

_____

_____

(2) In the table below, list details that Ridwan's story reveals about the Minangkabau culture.

Wedding Costumes	Food	Property Ownership

(3) Think about facts from Ridwan's story. Then, write two predictions about the cultures of Southeast Asia based on his story.

_____

_____

_____

_____

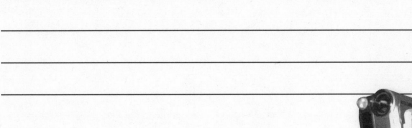

Name _____ Class _____ Date _____

Word Wise

Vocabulary Quiz Show Some quiz shows ask a question and expect the contestant to give the answer. In other shows, the contestant is given an answer and must supply the question. If the blank is in the question column, write the question that would result in the answer given. If the question is supplied, write the appropriate answer.

QUESTION

ANSWER

(1) What are Southeast Asia's seasonal winds called?

(1) _____

(2) _____

(2) typhoon

(3) What word describes a group of islands?

(3) _____

(4) _____

(4) tsunami

(5) What is the term given to a land area that is surrounded by water on three sides?

(5) _____

Name _____ Class _____ Date _____

Take Notes

Map Skills Use the maps in your book to make a key and to label the Places to Know on the outline map below.

Places to Know!

Physical Features	Cities
Mekong River	Jakarta
Malay Peninsula	Manila
Irrawaddy River	Hanoi
Red River	

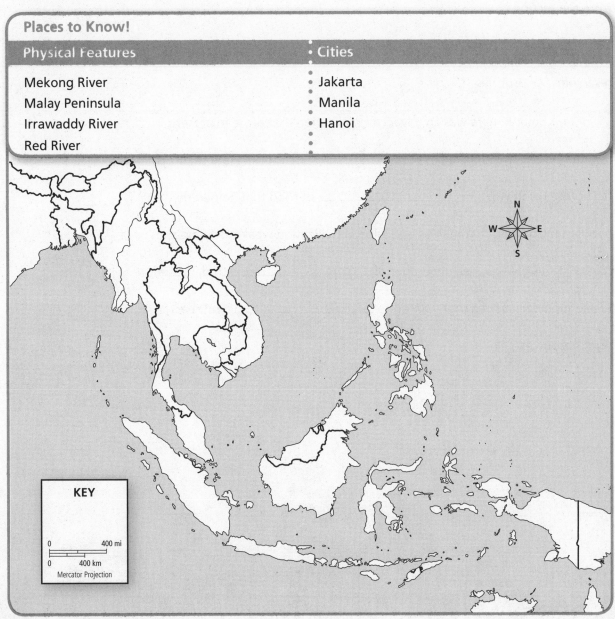

KEY

0 _____ 400 mi

0 _____ 400 km

Mercator Projection

Essential Question

Why did the geography of the region help create such a diverse population?

_____

_____

_____

Name _____ Class _____ Date _____

Word Wise

Word Bank Choose one word from the word bank to fill in each blank. When you have finished, you will have a short summary of important ideas from the section.

Word Bank

exploit   maritime
reservoirs   surplus

The Khmer Empire was an advanced civilization that arose in present-

day Cambodia. The Khmers built _____ to irrigate their rice

fields. The result was a(n) _____ of food that helped the

population to thrive. In time this agricultural civilization weakened, and the

coastal states grew powerful because of _____ trade. Later,

Western powers arrived that wanted to _____ Southeast

Asia's resources.

Name _____ Class _____ Date _____

Take Notes

Sequence Use what you have read about the history of Southeast Asia to complete the timeline below.

Timeline of Southeast Asian History	
100 B.C.	Co Loa conquered by China
A.D. 600	_____
	_____
1287	_____
	_____
1414	_____
	_____
1511	_____
	_____
1954	_____
	_____

Essential Question

How did Southeast Asians react to contact with many different religions?

_____

_____

_____

Word Wise

Words In Context For each question below, write an answer that shows your understanding of the boldfaced key term.

1 Why would some Indonesians prefer that their nation pursue **secular** policies?

_____

_____

_____

2 What is the attitude of Myanmar's **military junta** toward dissenters like Aung San Suu Kyi?

_____

_____

_____

3 Why is the Philippine government fighting **insurgency** on its islands in the south and east?

_____

_____

_____

4 What does the Islamic **separatist group** of the Philippines want?

_____

_____

_____

5 In what ways does **ASEAN** try to help Southeast Asia?

_____

_____

_____

Name _____ Class _____ Date _____

Take Notes

Main Idea and Details The topic headings in the table below match the headings in this section of your textbook. For each topic, write the overall main idea in the second column. Then, write two or three details that support the main idea in the third column.

Topic	Main Idea	Details
Southeast Asian Culture Today	Southeast Asia's position on trade routes has led to a blending of many cultures.	• Foreign merchants and immigrants arrived. • Different religious faiths came to the region and mixed with local beliefs.
Religion		
Governments and Citizens		
Population and Environment		
Diverse Economies		

? Essential Question

Why has "Unity in Diversity become the motto of Indonesia?

_____

_____

_____

What are the challenges of diversity?

Prepare to Write

Throughout this chapter, you have explored the Essential Question in your text, journal, and On Assignment at myWorldGeography.com. Use what you've learned to write an essay on the topic of the challenges of diversity in Southeast Asia. Keep in mind the region's many cultural traditions, religions, political systems, and languages. Think about how the region's geographical features attracted people from many lands. Consider, too, how Southeast Asia's history has contributed to these differences.

Workshop Skill: Revise Your Essay

Review the four steps of the writing process: (1) prewriting, (2) drafting, (3) revising, and (4) presenting. The first two steps require writing a thesis statement, an introduction, three body paragraphs, and a conclusion. Revising means carefully reading over a draft of your essay in order to correct and improve it.

In this lesson, you will learn how to revise your essay. Revision requires looking at the essay as a whole. It also involves a close look at each paragraph and sentence.

Use a Checklist Follow this checklist to revise your essay in an organized way. As you complete each task, check it off your list.

Polish Your Introduction and Thesis Statement Make sure that the opening of your essay is clear. It must catch your reader's attention.

_____ My introduction is interesting and easy to understand.

_____ My thesis statement is neither too general nor too specific.

Polish the Body of Your Essay and Concluding Paragraph Make sure that your paragraphs are logical and easy to follow.

_____ Each paragraph has a main idea and several supporting details.

_____ The transitions between paragraphs make sense.

_____ My conclusion is based on information in my essay.

Polish Your Sentences Make sure that each sentence is grammatically correct and interesting.

_____ Each sentence has a subject and a verb.

_____ My sentences are varied. There are simple sentences, compound sentences, and complex sentences.

Proofread Each Paragraph This step requires taking a close look at each sentence and each word. Use proofreading marks instead of rewriting.

_____ My sentences are free of grammar, punctuation, and capitalization errors.

Proofreading Marks

C̲	capitalize	ℓ̷	lowercase
ℓ̸	delete	⋀	comma
ro⌃k (insert)	insert	⊙	period

Here is a sample of a short paragraph that has been proofread. Changes have been made to increase sentence variety, too.

Diverse political systems create̷s different problems for the nations of

southeast asia. Myanmar's military junta forbids dissent. Sometimes

demonstrations erupt⌃, and leaders like Aun̷t San Suu Kyi get arrested. ⌃The

Philippines have a democracy with three bran̷ches of government. ⌃A

separatist group is rebelling against the government.

Now revise the following paragraph. Use proofreading marks to correct the errors in capitalization, punctuation, and spelling.

Religious deversity in the region sometimes leads to tension. Different

forms of Buddhism spread from india and china. Islam replaced Buddhism

and Hinduism in many of the region's islands. The philippines are mostly

Catholic and Insurgents are fighting for a separate Islamic State there. The

majority of Indonesia's mixed population is Moslem. However, the country's

secular government is tolerant.

Revise Your Essay
Use the checklists in this workshop and proofreading marks to revise your own essay. Then, rewrite your final draft on a new piece of paper.

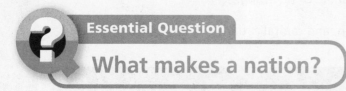

Name _____ Class _____ Date _____

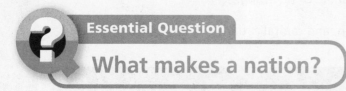

Essential Question

What makes a nation?

Preview Before you begin this chapter, think about the Essential Question. Understanding how the Essential Question connects to your life will help you understand the chapter you are about to read.

Connect to Your Life

1 Think about foreign nations that you have visited, read about, or have seen in television shows and movies. What makes those nations different from the United States?

Things That Make Nations Different From Each Other			
Institutions	• Geography	• Culture	• Other

Connect to the Chapter

2 Suppose you are going to start a new nation. What are the essential things that it would need? Before you read the chapter, flip through and note the red headings, maps, and other pictures. Record your ideas on the concept web below.

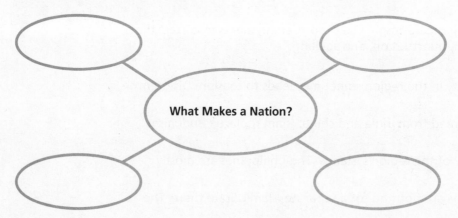

What Makes a Nation?

3 Read the chapter. Then connect each of the ideas you included in the web to an example from

Australia: _____ New Zealand: _____

Antarctica: _____ The Pacific Islands: _____

Name _____ Class _____ Date _____

Connect to myStory:
Jack Connects to His Culture

(1) List three customs your family follows that honors your background. Explain how these customs connect to who you are both as an individual and as a resident of the United States.

_____

_____

_____

(2) How does Jack make his Maori background an important part of his life? Fill in the table below with at least one example from each category.

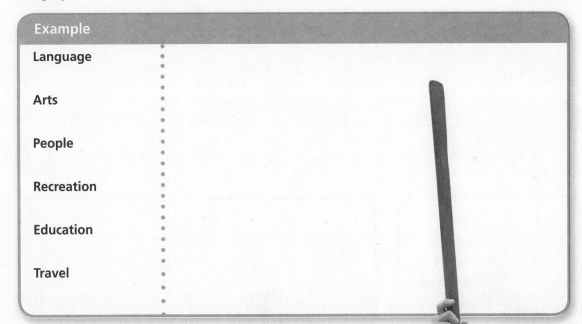

Example	
Language	
Arts	
People	
Recreation	
Education	
Travel	

(3) Jack's story explains that there has been increased interest in Maori culture in recent decades. How do you think this rebirth of Maori culture connects New Zealand's past and present?

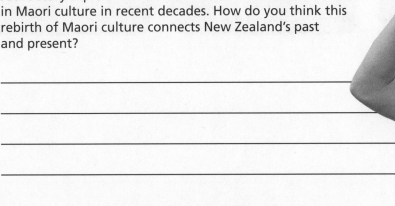

_____

_____

_____

_____

Word Wise

Vocabulary Quiz Show Some quiz shows ask a question and expect the contestant to give the answer. In other shows, the contestant is given an answer and must supply the question. If the blank is in the question column, write the question that would result in the answer given. If the question is supplied, write the appropriate answer.

QUESTION	ANSWER
① What explains the way parts of Earth's crust move and shift?	① _____
② _____	② atoll
③ What interior region of Australia is characterized by dry, low plains and plateaus?	③ _____
④ _____	④ coral reef

Name _____ Class _____ Date _____

Take Notes

Map Skills Use the maps in your book to make a key and to label the Places to Know on the outline map below.

Places to Know!

Physical Features	Countries
Great Barrier Reef	Papua New Guinea
Southern Alps	
Mount Kosciuszko	
Darling River	
Indian Ocean	

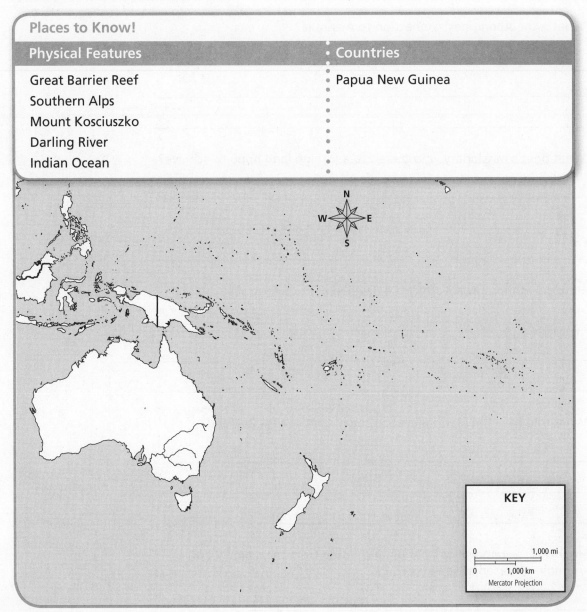

KEY

0 _____ 1,000 mi

0 _____ 1,000 km

Mercator Projection

Essential Question

How have climate, location, and resources affected the development of Australia, New Zealand, and the Pacific Islands?

_____

_____

_____

Word Wise

Words In Context For each question below, write an answer that shows your understanding of the boldfaced key term.

(1) What is the **Aborigines'** connection to Australia?

_____

_____

_____

(2) What does a **missionary** who travels to a foreign land hope to achieve?

_____

_____

_____

(3) How did **ethnocentrism** affect the development of Australia's culture?

_____

_____

_____

(4) What role have the **Maori** played in the history of New Zealand?

_____

_____

_____

(5) How was the removal of Aboriginal children from their families an example of forced **assimilation?**

_____

_____

_____

Name _____ Class _____ Date _____

Take Notes

Sequence The Pacific region was settled by a variety of groups. In the first box, describe the different peoples who migrated to Australia, New Zealand, and the Pacific islands. In the second box, describe the impact these people had on the region.

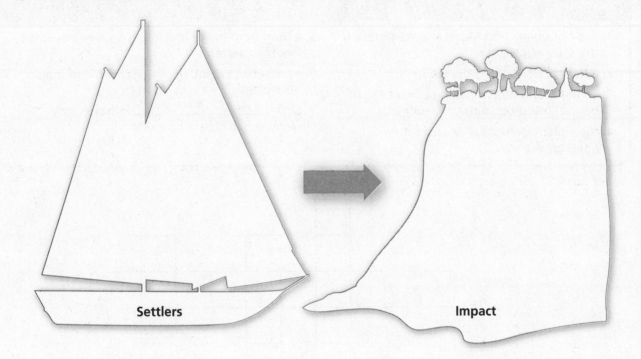

Settlers

Impact

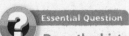 **Essential Question**

Does the history of colonization explain the formation of present-day nations in this region? Explain.

_____

_____

_____

Word Wise

Crossword Puzzle The clues describe key terms from this section. Fill in the numbered *Across* boxes with the correct key terms. Then, do the same with the *Down* clues.

Across	Down
1. the Aborigines and Maori are examples of this type of person	5. a long-term major change in an area's average weather patterns
2. a long period of very dry weather	6. a powerful explosive device capable of major destruction
3. an industry based on taking advantage of natural resources in the environment	7. a(n) _____ industry uses resources to create products
4. the violent overthrow of an existing government	

Name _____ Class _____ Date _____

Take Notes

Main Ideas and Details Use what you have read about modern Australia and the rest of the Pacific region to complete the graphic organizer. In the first box, write details about the region's people and culture. In the middle box, write details about countries' governments and economies. In the last box, write details about the region's environment.

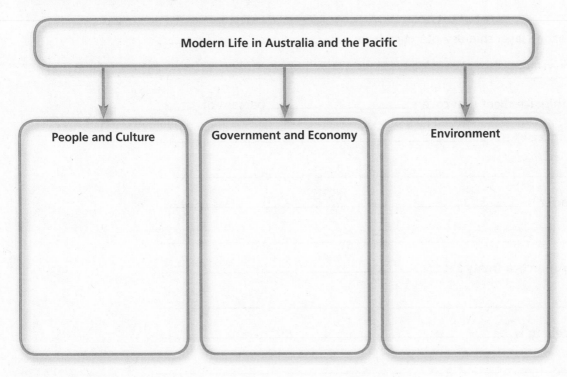

Modern Life in Australia and the Pacific

People and Culture

Government and Economy

Environment

Essential Question

How do governments and economies vary among the region's nations?

_____

_____

_____

Word Wise

Sentence Builder Complete the sentences using the information you learned in this section. Include terminal punctuation.

1. **Pack ice** forms in _____ and _____

   _____

2. The **ozone layer** shields Antarctica from _____

   _____

3. The thick **ice sheet** that covers _____ percent of

   Antarctica is _____

   _____

4. A **glacier** is _____

   _____

5. The **Antarctica Treaty** _____

   _____

6. An **iceberg** is _____

   _____

Name _____ Class _____ Date _____

Take Notes

Summarize Use what you have read about Antarctica to complete the flowchart below. In the first box, summarize Antarctica's physical geography. In the second box, summarize Antarctica's history of exploration and scientific research.

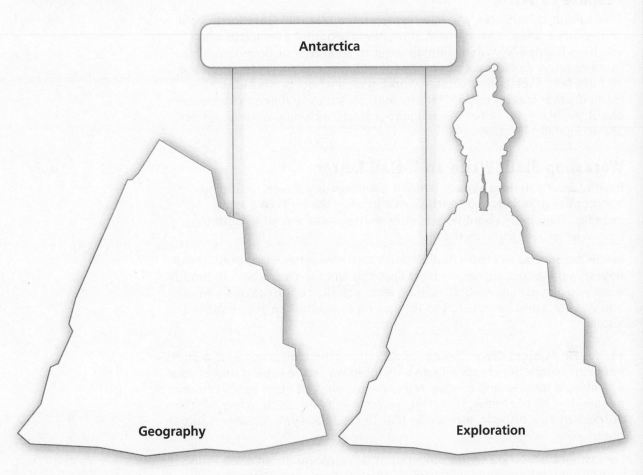

Antarctica

Geography

Exploration

Essential Question

Why have no nations formed in Antarctica?

_____

_____

_____

301

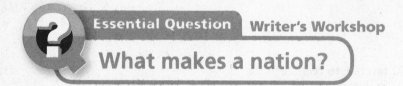

Essential Question Writer's Workshop

What makes a nation?

Prepare to Write

Throughout this chapter, you have explored the Essential Question in your text, journal, and On Assignment at myWorldGeography.com. Use what you have learned to write an e-mail letter to a minister or government representative at Australia's Department of Environment, Water, Heritage and the Arts. Explain that you are working on a school project about the elements that make a nation. Tell the minister that you'd like to know more about the places his or her department protects, including natural, historic, and indigenous locations.

Workshop Skill: Write an E-Mail Letter

Review what you have already learned about writing letters, including appropriate greetings and conclusions and what the body of a letter includes. Then think about how a letter written as an e-mail will differ from a letter sent through the mail.

In this lesson, you will learn how to write an e-mail letter. First, think about how to write a concise, clear subject line. You will then learn how to modify what you already know about writing letters to fit the format of an e-mail. You will also consider how to use formatting to strengthen your e-mailed letter.

Make the Subject Clear Unlike formal letters, there is no need for address headings before the greeting in an e-mail. However, the subject line of your e-mail must be clear and concise. Many people will not open e-mails from people they do not know. Therefore, your subject line needs to explain the purpose of your letter in such a way that the recipient will consider it safe to open.

For instance, if you are writing to a potential employer about a job listing, a good subject line would be *Response to ad for cashier in Saturday's newspaper.*

Write a clear, concise subject line for your e-mail to the Australian minister:

_____

Get Your Point Across Quickly Like its subject line, an e-mail letter needs to be as concise as possible. Most people have more difficulty processing information in a long e-mail than in reading a long hard-copy letter. Keep your e-mail short enough that the reader scrolls as little as possible.

Plan Your Paragraphs Suppose that your e-mail to the Australian minister is three paragraphs, as described in the table below. Record the main points you want to get across in each paragraph.

Paragraph 1: Briefly introduce yourself and your project.	
Paragraph 2: Describe the kind of information you would like the minister to give you about Australia. Explain how you will use this information.	
Paragraph 3: Provide your contact information and project deadline. Thank the minister for his or her time.	

Take Advantage of Technology Think about how to use your e-mail program's features to your advantage. For example, a spell-checker is helpful. You may wish to use formatting features like boldfacing and italics to make text stand out. Don't overuse these features. Avoid emoticons and casual abbreviations. Also, do not write words in solid capitals, as many people consider that rude in an e-mail.

Now, draft the second paragraph of your e-mail using your notes above. Circle instances where you would use features of your e-mail program, such as the spell-checker or formatting features.

_____

_____

_____

Be Ready for a Quick Reply Conclude your e-mail with appropriate thanks, complete contact information (such as your snail mail address and phone number), and your full name. There is no need to include your e-mail address since the recipient will probably just hit the reply button. The speed of e-mail means that you might receive a reply faster than you expected. Be prepared to write quick reply thanking him or her for the response.

Write Your E-mail Letter

Now use the information you jotted down in the table above to create a complete e-mail on a computer. Be sure your e-mail includes a clear subject line, a concise body, neat formatting, and a proper conclusion. E-mail it to a classmate "minister" for feedback.

Acknowledgments

Maps

XNR Productions, Inc.

Photography

2, Mike Agliolo/Corbis; 3, Saul Loeb/AFP/Getty Images; 4, L, Bill Curtsinger/National Geographic; R, Image Makers/Getty Images; 12, Jim Sugar/Corbis; 14, Indranil Mukherjee/AFP/Getty Images; 17, Wave RF/Photolibrary; 18, Galen Rowell/Corbis; 19, Jake Rajs/Getty Images; 21, Melanie Stetson Freeman/The Christian Science Monitor/Getty Images; 23, All Canada Photos/Alamy; 27, Bruno Morandi/age Fotostock; 29, SuperStock/age Fotostock; 32, ©2008 by Ira Lippke/Newscom; 33, PCL/Alamy; 35, istockphoto; 37, LB, Pearson; 38, GoGo Images Corporation/Alamy; 42, Stephane De Sakutin/AFP/Getty Images; 43, Matthew Ward/Dorling Kindersley; 45, Todd Gipstein/Corbis; 48, Kote Rodrigo/EFE/Corbis; 49, Jeff Greenberg/PhotoEdit; 51, Andy Crawford/Dorling Kindersley, Courtesy of the University Museum of Archaeology and Anthropology, Cambridge; 52, Bettmann/Corbis; 53, O. Louis Mazzatenta/National Geographic; 55, El Comercio Newspaper, Dante Piaggio/AP Images; 57, BR, Pearson; 60, Dynamic Graphics/age Fotostock; 63, moodboard/Corbis; 67, Pearson; 68, John E Marriott/Getty Images; 70, Nathan Benn/Alamy; 77, Pearson; 82, Paul E. Rodriguez/Newscom; 83, L. Zacharie/Alamy; 88, Reuters/Enrique De La Osa (CUBA); 90, The Art Archive/Archaeological Museum Tikal Guatemala/Gianni Dagli Orti; 97, Pearson; 102, Photoshot Holdings Ltd/Bruce Coleman; 103, Suraj N. Sharma/Dinodia Picture Agency; 107, Pearson; 110, *Sebastian de Benalcazar (1480–1551)*, Eladio Sevilla II (fl. 1950), Oil on canvas/Museo Municipal, Quito, Ecuador/Index/The Bridgeman Art Library; 112, Steve Allen/Getty Images; 117, Pearson; 120, Reuters/Jamil Bittar; 122, Marcelo Rudini/Alamy; 128, Nick Nicholls/The British Museum/Dorling Kindersley; 132, Museum of History of Sofia, Sofia, Bulgaria/Archives Charmet/Bridgeman Art Library; 134, Geoff Dann/Dorling Kindersley; 140, Philip Gatward/Dorling Kindersley; 142, Joel W. Rogers/Corbis; 144, Getty Images/De Agostini Editore Picture Library; 146, Bettmann/Corbis; 148, Bettmann/Corbis; 153, Pearson; 166, Dean Conger/Corbis; 168, Carlos Nieto/age Fotostock; 173, Pearson; 174, Sovfoto/Eastfoto; 176, Charles & Josette Lenars/Corbis; 178, Iain Masterton/Alamy Images; 183, TR, Pearson; BR, Pearson; 184, George Steinmetz/Corbis; 186, Joan Pollock/Alamy; 194, SuperStock; 196, The Granger Collection, New York; 198, Pearson; 203, Pearson; 204, Franck Guiziou/Hemis/Corbis; 208, Olivier Martel/Corbis; 214, Ed Kashi/Aurora Photos; 216, Georg Gerster/Photo Researchers, Inc.; 217, The London Art Archive/Alamy; 223, Pearson; 236, The Art Archive/Dagli Orti; 238, AFP/Getty Images; 243, Pearson; 244, R, dbimages/Alamy; L, Shamil Zhumatov/Reuters; 248, Tim Brakemeier/dpa/Corbis; 253, Pearson; 258, S. Forster/Alamy; 263, Pearson; 264, Bruno Morandi/Robert Harding World; 266, Peter Gridley/Getty Images; 268, Yin Hai/epa/Corbis; 273, Pearson; 274, AP Photo/Yonhap, Yu Hyung-je; 276, dbimages/Alamy; 283, Pearson; 286, Yi Lu/Corbis; 293, Pearson; 294, George Steinmetz/Corbis; 298, Shutterstock; 299, Jonathan Marks/Corbis.